"Yours for ̄
A Romanc̣

Edited by John H Rumsby

Published by

Huddersfield Local History Society
2014

"Yours for Eternity"
A Romance of the Great War

© John H. Rumsby

Published by
Huddersfield Local History Society
8, Station Road
Golcar
Huddersfield
HD7 4ED

www.huddersfieldhistory.org.uk

ISBN 978-0-9509134-9-0

Designed by
JMP Creative Production
113 Lidget Street, Lindley, Huddersfield HD3 3DR

Printed and bound in Great Britain by
Charlesworth Press
Flanshaw Way, Flanshaw Lane, Wakefield WF2 9LP

Contents

Acknowledgements

This book would not have been possible without the generosity of the finder of these letters, who not only rescued them from an attic, but so freely made them available for study and publication. I am also very grateful to the following individuals and groups who have contributed their enthusiastic help and support and, where necessary, given their permission for the reproduction of images:

Pauline and John Ainley; Judith Atkinson; Amanda Booth; Robert Carter; Jane Chesworth, BBC Leeds; the publications group of the Huddersfield Local History Society; the staff of Kirklees Library Service; the staff of Kirklees Museums Service; Pauline Marples; Catherine Mowat; the staff of the National Archives; Cyril Pearce; Barbara Smith; David Verguson; the staff of the West Yorkshire Archive Service; Chris Yeates.

Introduction

A few years ago a friend of my daughter was exploring her newly-purchased house in Birkby, Huddersfield, West Yorkshire. In the attic she found a rusty tin box. Inside, wrapped in an old newspaper, was a bundle of about 150 letters and postcards, in their original envelopes. A quick look at some of the contents revealed them to be the correspondence between a Huddersfield soldier and his sweetheart, written between 1914 and 1916. The soldier, Henry Coulter, lived in Marsh, and his girlfriend, Lucy Townend, lived in the house where the letters were found. Knowing of my interest in military and local history, the discoverer generously lent the letters to me. I have transcribed the letters, and added a few notes about the people, places and events to which they refer. However, for the most part the letters speak for themselves.

The letters contain no great military revelations, new facts or insights, although Henry did serve in one of the famous 'Bantam' battalions, formed from men of short stature. Most of them were written whilst Henry was in training in various camps in England. Only the last few were sent whilst he was on active service in France. He does however give us a picture of a soldier's life from the point of view of an ordinary young man who before the Great War started would probably never have dreamed of joining the army. His account of his soldiering was written to entertain and reassure his sweetheart, not to satisfy future military historians. He was much more concerned with expressing his love, in often painfully intimate terms, for his 'Beauty,' Lucy, whom he refers to several times as his future wife. He signs most of his letters (along with numerous kisses) 'Yours for Eternity, Henry.' More mundane matters − requests for a razor, a mirror, tins of Dubbin − take us to the local world of Huddersfield,

Mitre Street, Marsh, about 1910. Henry lived in Marsh Fold, the next street, so this scene would have been familiar to him. (Kirklees Image Archive k002584)

a reasonably prosperous industrial town with a wide variety of local retail businesses, entertainment establishments, and social communities based on church or chapel.

Henry and Lucy were members of Gledholt Wesleyan Methodist Church, Westbourne Road, Marsh. This church had been opened in October 1890, with a large Sunday school (replacing an earlier building) added in 1908. It is still used for Christian worship. At the beginning of the twentieth century churches and chapels played a much greater role in society than they do today. They were not only places of worship, but centres for many other social activities. Some were religious, such as bible classes and choirs, but there were also lectures, sports clubs, socials and concerts. All this appealed to young people, large numbers of whom had grown up attending Sunday school. Henry was a member of the Young Men's Bible Class, and seems to have delivered comic monologues, which he composed himself, at social events. However, the couple obviously enjoyed the full range of popular entertainment that a town the size of Huddersfield could offer in 1914: popular theatre, music hall, and especially the fast-growing cinema. The only exception was that they were unlikely to have frequented Huddersfield's numerous public houses: Methodism was a staunch supporter of the temperance movement. Like their twenty-first century successors, these two young people had their favourite celebrities; in their case Charlie Chaplin, George Formby Senior, and especially Gladys Cooper. Walks in Greenhead Park, or along their favourite lane, with plenty of 'kisses and cuddles' was a popular pastime for this young couple.

In short, these letters are much more about two young people in a Yorkshire town very much in love, than about the great events that commenced in 1914, that were so tragically to tear them apart.

The Correspondents

Henry Coulter was born in Ardwick, Manchester on 2 November 1891.[1] His father, also called Henry, was a grocer's assistant. His mother Lucy died in 1896 and his father remarried in 1898. This is possibly why Henry was living with his father's widowed sister, Mrs Luke (Adeline) Schofield, at number 12 Westbourne Road, Marsh, Huddersfield.[2] Adeline's husband had died in 1900. Henry obviously had a close relationship with his aunt, whom he called 'Ma.' He was educated at Spring Grove Council School, Huddersfield. In 1914 he was working as a clerk at Huddersfield Corporation's Tramways Department, and his letters are well-written in a clear and articulate style. He probably met his sweetheart at Gledholt Methodist Church, which is only a few yards from where he was living. Henry's letters present him as a likeable, loving young man with a quirky sense of humour, obviously immersed in the popular culture of the day (note his quotations from advertising slogans), and always anxious for weekend passes so that he could see his 'Lu' again.

Lucy Townend was born in Worksop in 1898. In 1914 she was living in a small terraced house in Tanfield Road, Birkby, with her parents Charles (born in Worksop 1870 – died Huddersfield 1929) and Emily (born Sheffield c.1874 – died Huddersfield before 1929), and two younger brothers Henry and Alan. A sister, Edith, seems to have died as a young child. In 1914 Lucy's father was working as a domestic chauffeur in Huddersfield, but when Lucy was younger he had been a head groom on an estate at Morthern near Rotherham. When she was aged ten, Lucy had bravely rescued her little brother Henry from an icy pond, an event recorded in a newspaper clipping preserved with the correspondence:

Gledholt Wesleyan Methodist Church, about 1910. The new Sunday school is on the right.
(Kirklees Image Archive k002586)

MORTHEN[3]

A CHILD'S BRAVERY. An interesting account of child heroism reaches us from the obscure hamlet of Morthen, which tells of the bravery of a little girl of the tender age of ten years, who saved her little brother from drowning. It transpires that four young children – three boys and a girl – whose ages ranged from 3 ½ to 10 years, belonging to Mr Charles Townend, head groom of Mr A.M. Eadon, of Morthen Hall, on Sunday wandered towards Morthen pond for the purpose of going on the ice. One of the boys, aged seven, was deputed to test the strength of the ice, but it promptly gave way, and the little fellow was quickly immersed. Fortunately, however, the girl had the presence of mind to realise the danger, and without demur went into the water, and after a struggle was successful in bringing her brother safely to the bank side. Such a noble act is certainly worthy of noting and the circumstances should be brought [before?] the Royal Humane Society for consideration.

At the time Henry was courting her, Lucy was about sixteen, and worked in a shoe shop, probably belonging to the Huddersfield Industrial Society Ltd (the 'Co-op'). She described herself as a 'careless, thoughtless girl' until she met Henry, and her relationship with her parents was occasionally stormy. Fewer of Lucy's letters survive than Henry's, and the handwriting, spelling and punctuation are somewhat uncertain, suggesting that she may have left school at thirteen or fourteen. Nevertheless the letters were written from the heart, and express her feelings clearly.

The Letters

For reasons of space some of Henry's letters have had to be omitted, and others cut down (indicated by '…'). All Lucy's surviving letters have been included. In most cases Henry and Lucy's long and loving greetings and farewells have also been omitted. The text of what has been included has however been printed exactly as it was written, including any spelling mistakes. Most of Henry's letters written during his army service are on headed notepaper which he acquired from one of the organisations who supplied various comforts for soldiers' welfare: the Young Men's Christian Association (YMCA), the Salvation Army or the Soldiers' Christian Association. Some however were written on notepaper bearing the crest of the West Yorkshire Regiment. The correspondence illustrates how frequent and reliable the Royal Mail was at this time: with five deliveries a day, Henry could expect a letter to arrive in Birkby the same day, even when sent from an army camp in the countryside.

FROM HENRY, WESTBOURNE ROAD, MARSH, 31 OCTOBER 1914

Dear Little Girl,

Sorry to have had to disappoint you this evening, but I really could not get down. My cold wouldn't let me. And it is such a beast of a night too. But I am dying nicely, thank you. (Sorry, I mean *doing* nicely. Quite a slip on my part I assure you.) But to return to the tragedy. I had a good dose of Salts of Lemon last night & two doses of Rat-poison this morning. So I'm 'progressing favourably' as they say at the Infirmary. I will see you to-morrow (Sunday) night at 8 o'clock as usual if that is convenient. That is; 'Cold' & Weather permitting. However, I think I'll come to a conclusion & return to my reading of the 'Fatal Thirteen,' until bed-time.[4] With lots of "Luv' & heaps of [kisses] Yours ever, Henry.

PS Don't forget the Photo.

FROM HENRY, CHRISTMAS CARD DECEMBER 1914

Printed in gold throughout.
With the Compliments of the Season and all Good Wishes for a Bright and Prosperous New Year.
From Henry Coulter.
12 Westbourne Road, Marsh, Huddersfield. Christmas, 1914.

FROM HENRY, WESTBOURNE ROAD, MARSH, 23 JANUARY 1915

Sorry I cannot come down to see you to-night but I have been in bed the biggest part of to-day. I did not get up until 5 o'clock & I have been to the Doctor since then. He says I have a very bad throat; but that I went to him in time, or else I should probably have had another dose of 'Quinzies.'[5] What a deliverance. If you care to go to Miss Noel's party it will be quite all right to me. It will pass the evening on for you; but if you do go, don't stop too late. There's a darling. I am sorry that I shall not be able to see you to-morrow (Sunday) but it can't be helped, can it? (That's the worst of these cheap German throats, there so unreliable.) I have been composing again to-night, just to while away the time, & am enclosing it for your kind supervision. (Passed by Censor.)[6] If you have left that rotten stuff of mine at the Office, it will have to stop there until I go; but if not, then keep it until I see you again. (Or better still, bury it in the garden at dead of night. It will be a far, far better thing than you ever did before.) Please excuse pencil; also scribble. Write me a line or two to-morrow if you will. Kind regards to Mother;
With the usual 'L of L' & 'Heaps of [kisses]' Yours ever, Henry.

FROM HENRY, WESTBOURNE ROAD, MARSH, 25 JANUARY 1915

I duly received your welcome letter this dinner-time[7] & was glad to hear from you. With regard to your enquiries; I am dying nicely: (doing nicely) & am going to 'Biz.' in the morning. My

Rushworth's corner, about 1914. A popular place to meet friends in town.
(Kirklees Image Archive k006410)

HUDDERSFIELD WAR HOSPITAL MAGAZINE.

Our Pen Service.

We get on intimate terms with every pen we stock—become acquainted with their mechanism and adaptability to different classes of work. Don't be afraid of troubling us—we're looking for this kind of trouble. Nibs may be changed as often as necessary.

Full Range of Swans, Onotos, & Watermens.

The Westgate is a useful pen at a low price - With 14ct. gold nibs   -   -   -   **3/6**

The Blackbird, made by the same Firm as the famous Swan, a very reliable pen   -   -   -   **6/-**

The Corona, very handy for soldiers, fitted with ink pellets for making ink   -   -   -   -   **4/6**

Corona Stylo, in black or tan, fitted with patent ink trap   -   -   -   -   -   -   **5/-**

Rushworths Ltd.

The Corner of

Westgate & John Williams St

Huddersfield

Advertisement for Rushworth's stores. Note the Corona pen – 'very handy for soldiers.'
(Huddersfield War Hospital Magazine 1917)

throat is still sore but I shall have to make a start sometime, so the sooner the better. I am just about sick of being in. Fancy! three whole days & not seeing a soul except Ma & our 'Dreadnought.'[8] Bless his ugly black face. I'm sure its going paler with worry. Have you written the story out yet? It's about time it was published. What a surprise our kind friends at Gledholt will have when they see it in 'Yes or No' Novels or something like that. I hope you had a good time at the party. With regard to our friend 'Burnham;' how awfully good of him to give you a good character. Do you think you could give him one? I wonder. I have been thinking out more songs. In fact I've material enough to fill a 'Francis, Day & Hunter's' & a 'Feldman's' Annual[9] & still have enough to start a couple of Pantomimes with. 'Oh! What a Brain.' (I haven't room for 'Dirty Water & Sawdust' so have to write 'Brain.') I am just beginning to wonder what's the matter with it. I have written a new 'Monologue' entitled:- 'Cuthbert, fetch the Landlord, Tommy's eating all the jam.' Sorry I mean 'Silly Questions.' I'm sure you'll like it: It's such a pathetic little thing. But I'll bring it down with me to-morrow night (Tuesday). I shall come down about 7-30 so please stay in & then I'll whistle. I mean Tanfield Road not Rushworth's Corner.[10] It's no use you going on there; is it? Please excuse the scribble & the erasing as my hand trembles yet.

With fondest love, yours ever, Henry.

FROM HENRY, WESTBOURNE ROAD, MARSH, 29 MAY 1915, 1-30 AM

Sorry to disappoint you again, but I shall not be able to be with you to-night as arranged as I have to come on duty again at 1 o'clock to work my late shift.[11] Our Cashier says he has no-one else to take it; so as usual it falls on 'your humble.' However, don't worry; use 'Sunlight Soap.' I am going to Leeds again this morning by the 9-25 train; but have to be back in Hudd. again by 12 o'clock so I have my work set hav'nt I. However

I will see you by Shaw & Hallas' Boot Shop[12] in Westgate at 9-30 to-night certain. With the usual 'Lots of Luv & Krowds of Kisses…'

This trip to Leeds was so that Henry could enlist, which he did on this day, in the 17th Battalion West Yorkshire Regiment. There had been a huge recruiting drive in Huddersfield on 8 May 1915, involving over 12,000 men of the 38th Division. It is possible that this was what persuaded Henry to enlist. However, it seems certain that he was under the army's regulation minimum height of 5 feet 3 inches, and had tried to enlist before but had been turned down. 'Bantam' battalions like the 17th (2nd Leeds) West Yorkshires were allowed to take men between 5 feet and 5 feet 3 inches in height. Leeds was working hard to recruit men: by the end of April 1915 30,000 men had enlisted in the city.[13] Henry must have been describing his own frustrating experiences of trying to join up in a regulation-sized regiment when he wrote the following monologue:

MONOLOGUE, DATED 26 JANUARY 1915

The Recruit.

1.
One morn whilst getting out of bed,
A notion entered Tommy's head.
'That to the Drill Hall he would go.'
'And 'list against our German foe.'
2.
When he got there the Sentry said,
'Halt! Who goes there? Quick, or you're dead.'
But Tommy said 'It's only me,
'A Soldier Sir, I want to be.'
3.
'Well pass inside:' the Sentry smiled.
But then the Sergeant, Tom espied.

And stood with fear, just by the door.
(He'd been so awfully brave before.)
4.
'Hullo my lad, What d'you want here?'
'You'd better run off home I fear.'
But Tommy gave his only plea,
'A Soldier Sir, I want to be.'
5.
'Alright my lad,' the Sergeant said.
'How tall are you?' Tom shook his head.
'The Regulation's five foot three.'
'Just stand up there & then I'll see.'
6.
The Sergeant measured Tom & then
He hum'd & haw'd, & hum'd again.
'I'm sorry lad, you'll have to go.'
'You're 5 ft. 2: *Go home & grow.*'
HE WENT.

FROM HENRY, RAIKSWOOD CAMP, SKIPTON, 31 MAY 1915[14]

I have arrived all right about 4-30 & am liking all right up
to now. We are stationed in Huts having removed from Ilkley
during the last day or two. I have just had my tea. Pineapple
chunks & bread & 'Margarine.' (They make tea in buckets
here.)[15] Also I have filled my bedding & pillow with straw. It
is a lovely place; all surrounded with woods. I think this is all
for the present. Will write again when I get my number & full
address.

*Raikswood (or Raikeswood) Camp was built in January 1915 on an exposed
site on the top of a hill to the north of Skipton, next to what is now Salisbury
Street. It was built and paid for by Bradford's Citizens' Army League to house*

New Recruits Foreign Service 5th West Riding Regiment, St George's Square Huddersfield, 5th September 1914 (Huddersfield Local Studies Library)

the 'Bradford Pals,' the 16th and 18th Battalions, West Yorkshire Regiment. There were 36 huts for the men, with others for officers, baths, canteen, cookhouse, stables, and an institute which held 500 men for concerts and recreation. By February 1915 the camp held 1300 men. When the Bradford Pals moved to a camp at Ripon in May, the Bantams moved in. The camp eventually became a Prisoner-of-War camp, and was dismantled in October 1919.[16]

FROM HENRY, RAIKSWOOD CAMP, 2 JUNE 1915

I hope you received my letter alright. I am getting along very nicely at present; but I have had a time & no error. The grub here is getting better though. I will just try & give you a description of what I mean; since I came here. To begin with, the place itself is lovely. Surrounded by trees, it is just like a garden city. There are about 45 huts altogether & all nic-named. For example:- 'Keystone Palace,' 'Carry on Cottage,' '10 Dow[n]ing St' & 'Midland Hotel.'[17] The last named is where I am billeted. They are a very fair lot of fellows though, taking them on the whole. On Monday night I slept on a straw mattress on the floor & caught cold through the draught at the bottom of the door. But I have got a wooden folding bedstead since. (What a contrast to a white bed!) Then next the grub sickened me. I did without from Monday morning until this morning & then I had some fat bacon & tomato juice. I had to, I was starving. (That, on the menu, would be termed 'Bacon & Tomatoes.') But is it? Not in my estimation. But I am getting more used to it now & can eat it without a shudder. The days programme yesterday was, Bugle goes at 6 o'clock, go on parade at 6-30. After that drill until 7-30; then go into breakfast until 9 o'clock. Then I went to see about my uniform. (The rest did more drilling.) I have two uniforms & enough other clothing to last me 12 months. Then dinner (pardon the word) at 12 o'clock until 2 o'clock. Then parade again at two & drill until four. Then tea, & that completes the day's programme. I went to the Pictures last night with Frank Crosland & saw Charlie Chaplin in 'Charlie's New Job.' You have to be in by 9-15 though, or else its five days 'C.B.' (Confined to Barracks) besides an hour's pack drill each night.[18] So the penalty is far greater than the crime. Lights out at 10 o'clock & then you get to sleep. (if you can.) I felt properly sick of everything yesterday & would have given worlds to be with you again. But there, I am not going to complain. I am going to stick it & I think it seems likely to improve. And now I will tell you today's programme. No early parade this morning; but paraded at 9 o'clock instead & went a route march to Bolton Abbey. Five & a half miles each way, making a total of eleven. We took our dinners with us & got back about five o'clock & then dismissed. Will you ask Ma if she will make me a cake & then you can send it. There's a darling if you will. (And you couldn't refuse could you?) We only get very plain food. Your Ma I mean. And give her my love & my kind regards to your father. And tell him I am going to stick it. (As I write these words tears come into my eyes. I don't know why; but there I always was a baby.) To-morrow we are having a day's holiday in honour of the King's Birthday. To-night it is fire drill at 10-30 p.m. so it should be exciting shouldn't it? I will tell you all about it next time though. Well darling I think that is all that I can think of at present but keep a brave heart & a smiling face for it will all come right in time. So write back to me won't you my 'beauty?'

Pte H. Coulter (1570)

Hut 43, 'E. Co,' 17th West Yorks;

Raikswood Camp, Skipton.

FROM LUCY, 3 JUNE 1915

Thank you so much for your two letters, though the one I got this morning nearly broke my heart. Oh Henry dear I am sorry for you I could cry when I think about it all. I do feel lonely without you it seems an age since you went away. how I worked on Monday afternoon I dont know, if I could just come too you for half an hour I should feel heaps better but that cannot be and I ought not to talk to you in this gloomy strain you have quite enough to put up with. I am sending a small parcel by the same post as this letter but I have an idea that the letter will reach you first if that is so look out for the parcel, it wont be long afterwards. I went for a walk with Marion on Wednesday afternoon, but oh I did miss you, I feel as if I dont care whether we close at seven or ten or whether we have half holiday or not. On Monday night Marion said No Henry at the bottom of Westgate to-night, I knew that only too well. I went to the Palace[19] last night (Wed) with father and mother we sat right up in that top corner you know and got there for the end of the first turn, just like dad that what! but although it is a fair week I felt miserable and my thoughts were at Skipton where they have been every day since you went. The stick you gave me Henry dear is up in a corner of my bedroom with my umbrella mounting guard over it just as you would guard me if you were here. You tell me to keep a brave & smiling face but oh what a task I have cried many times since you went and your photograph smiling at me so longingly from the dressing table as been a witness to it all. I feel just now as if I could lay down my pen and sob my heart out but I know you would not like me too do that. I hope you will like the contents of the parcel, and if there is anything you fancy you might let me know I shall have a better idea what too send then. Well Henry Walter Waterworth as not enlisted after all the Y.M.C.A. people would not let him so Amy will be glad. Bertie Sheard was in our shop on Wednesday morning, and he stared me through, Oh and I saw little Willie[20] on Wed and he asked if I had heard from you he said your Ma was up at their house on Monday night, and he gave me his girl's address so I shall write too her now. I went up to Gledholt on Tuesday night and am going again to-night am trying too be good you see. time I did isn't it. Well Henry dear cheer up and remember choose what comes there's a little girl in Huddersfield loving you all the time and longing for the time when you will come over if only for a short while. I am glad you saw Charlie Chaplin that would at any rate seem too you like an old friend in a strange land. I dont think I have any more to say. only that I watch for the post man every morning for your letters are all I have too look forward too. Please excuse scribble dear but my hand is not quite steady just now. Mother sends her best love she is very sorry for you dear and she feels it nearly as much as I do

The Palace Theatre, Kirkgate. A photograph taken before it was completely rebuilt in the 1930s.
(Kirklees Image Archive k004174)

if aching hearts could fetch you back you would not stay there long. But still we must hope for the best so I will close with fondest love.

From your loving little Sweetheart Lu.

PS Will send you photo as soon as I get them. Write soon as possible wont you but then I know you will. Lu.

FROM HENRY, RAIKSWOOD CAMP, 5 JUNE 1915

Many thanks for your kind letter which I received on Friday morning. Also the parcel which was glorious. It was very very kind of you & Mother to send it & I thank you very much. I have about four chums at my end of the hut so I gave them a little. You won't mind will you? It is nearly all done now worse luck. And now I will tell you about my doings since Wednesday night. I had just got to the fire drill I believe. We turned in about the usual time & the bugle went for 'lights out.' (10 o'clock) It started to rain about then & when the bugle went for fire drill at about eleven; it was pouring down. But we turned out to a man & paraded for half an hour in the rain and darkness. (Lovely wasn't it?) On Thursday we had a day's holiday in honour of the King's Birthday. Frank & I went to see Skipton Castle which dates back to the year dot. At night we went to a concert in the 'Y.M.C.A.' given by a troupe of artists such as you & I have seen at the palace. The 'Zig-Zags' they were called. Yesterday morning (Friday) we were inspected by the new Colonel & I stood to attention (for inspection) for nearly two hours, in the hot sun. There are nearly 1,600 here & he inspected every one. My words & it was warm. In the afternoon we had Swedish drill[21] for an hour, & was running up & down a field & jumping forms etc. (More warm work.) This morning (Sat.) we have no parades at all, but have to be up at 6-30 as usual. We clean up our huts etc., for inspection & then we have done for the day. That is about 10 o'clock. I have taken a place to-day in the Quarter Master's Office as they are very short of clerks here, & have to make out passes for leave & Railway Warrants & other clerking work. So you see I can't leave the ink alone can I? But I am only on trial until Monday so we shall have to see how things go on. I got a box of things from Ma this morning & will write to her to-morrow. How is the inevitable Teddy & Willie getting along? Have you seen them lately? Remember me to Marion & all the girls; boys I mean. Also to your Mother & give her my love. I am rapidly getting into good condition & my face is quite sunburnt. I think this is about all at present as I hear the bugle sounding for tea. So good bye my darling & think of me in your prayers won't you?

With my fondest Love, yours for ever, Henry.

PS Write back soon.

My Darling Little Girl,

Just a few lines in reply to your last letter which I received quite safely & which cheered me up so. I received your 'Examiner'[22] this dinner-time & it felt good to read about something of home. (Whenever I think of home or you, it always makes tears come into my eyes; & I am not the only one here by a long way. You would be surprised to see some of our most roughest fellows break down when we talk about home.) But there, this is to be a cheerful letter not a funeral. I hope you received the small present I sent you, quite safely. I forgot to say, though, that the White-Horse on the brooch is the mascot of the 17th West Yorks.[23] We all wear it on our Caps in the form of a badge; & it is said to be recognised as the oldest mascot of its kind in England. I hope you will like it & wear it for me my darling. It will be a constant reminder that someone, whom you love very dearly, is trying his level best to do his best for King & Country. However, we'll get on with the 'washing' as the saying is. This is a cheerful letter I believe. Last Sunday morning I had to miss 'Church Parade' as I was working in the office until tea-time; but at night Frank & I went for a stroll in the woods. On Monday we had the usual routine but at night we went to see our old friend Chas. Chaplin in 'Charlie's Night Out' & it was a screamer & no mistake. But perhaps you will have it over there before long. Last night we went into the woods again & fell asleep under the trees. I have been thinking about you a lot to-day my beauty. More than usual I think. But it was the day I suppose. We had a rest this afternoon for about half an hour (3 o'clock to 3-30) & as I lay on my back in the grass; I thought 'I wonder what my Lu is doing now? Gone to hear the Band I suppose.[24] The pride of all the boys & the envy of all the girls.' But there I mustn't tease you my dearest. You have enough to bear. I would give worlds to have you with me to-night, if only for an hour. Just to take you into Skipton Woods & cuddle you & smother you with kisses. But I am storing them all up for when I come home again. I have not yet written to Luke, but will do so when I have more time. I seem to be quite busy at present, but the novelty is begining to wear off & I am missing you more than ever now. You see you were my constant companion at home, my sweetheart. But there its time I pulled myself together, & not let my pen run away with my feelings. I forgot to say that I came out of the Office yesterday, until I can learn a few drills, but am going back again after. I think it does me more good out in the open besides. Many thanks for your promise of a cake. I received a cake & box of buns from Ma the other day, but they are all gone now. I think I have told you all the news this time so must come to an end. Give my best love to Mother (not *the* best) & remember me to your father & the boys,

FROM HENRY, RAIKSWOOD CAMP, 10 JUNE 1915

Just a short note to thank you for the parcel containing the cake (not forgetting the pencil & re-fills) which I received quite safely this morning. I am sure it is very good of you & I don't know how to thank you & Mother enough for your kindness. I am glad you liked your present; but it is nothing to what I should have liked to have sent you, if I had not been away. I am pleased to hear that Willie Brier is thinking of joining the colours. Tell him to come over here & we'll try & make a man of him: the same as they are trying to do to me. I have heard to-day that we are going to Coldersdale[25] (nr Ripon) on Monday, so when you write to me this week-end, post it not later than Sunday night. I do not know definate, but I have got it on good authority. Please excuse the pencil, but I am trying the one you sent me. It writes lovely & you are such a darling to think of it. But its just like you, beauty, to think of what I should need. Kindly remember me to Marion & Miss Blackshaw & all enquiring friends.

PS If we should happen to move, I will let you know as soon as I can. H.

FROM HENRY, RAIKSWOOD CAMP, 12 JUNE 1915

Many thanks, once again, for your long & loving letter which I received quite safely this morning. I do not know that I have much news to tell you this time except that it is a boiling hot day & that I have been sweating like a bull. I'm sure, if this weather goes on, that I shall be rendered down to a grease-spot, or else where the grease-spot has been. However, to get to business. I hope you will have a good day at the Anniversary to-morrow & hope you will clear £50 collections.[26] I was also very, very glad to learn that you had been up to see Ma on Thursday evening, & that you had promised to go to tea on Sunday. It is very good of you my darling & I thank you from the bottom of my heart. You will be such good company my beauty & it will cheer her up. I had a lovely parcel from her this morning containing some things of mine & more grub. And whilst on the subject of grub, tell your Ma that the cake was lovely. We had it for supper last night & the fellows said it was grand. I am enclosing you a P.O.[27] for 1/- as I want you to do a little errand on Monday for me if you will. (And I *know* you will my sweetheart.) I want you to slip into Heaton's (John Wm St Shop)[28] & ask him to give you one of those razors he has at 9d. each. Tell him who it's for & he will know the kind I mean. Then send it on to me by Monday night's post. The other 3d. will pay for the postage; & you can send me another loving letter besides. There are plenty of rumours going about that we are leaving next week. Some say Coldersdale, some Bradford, some Wales & some even to India. By the time we've been round the lot the War will be over I think. But just write

'Ablutions' – washing facilities, at Ripon Training Camp. Henry must have encountered similar conditions at Raikswood Camp, Skipton. (Private collection)

as usual, as it's no good believing anything, until I get to know definate. I am enclosing you a photo of the Y.M.C.A. hut here, where we write all our letters. I am sorry I cannot get one of the camp, but they do not allow them to be taken…

FROM HENRY, RAIKSWOOD CAMP, 15 JUNE 1915

Many, many thanks for your sweet letter (and parcel) which I received this morning; but oh! my 'beauty,' how lonely you must feel. I have read your letter over, several times to-day & it has brought tears to my eyes every time. How I feel for you darling. Sometimes, I begin to wonder if I have done right in leaving you; to try & do my little bit. (For I miss you just as much as you miss me, & feel quite as lonely, only in a different way.) But when we go out on the march & the whole battalion

(1,600 men) swing along the road, & the people cheer & shout; then I know, deep down in my heart, that I have done right, & it makes me feel glad that I have sacrificed leaving you to try & do my share. So you understand my feelings, don't you, sweetheart? I am glad the Anniversary went off alright, & the collection was very fair. With regard to the 'Roll of Honour,' I leave that in your hands, as you think it fit to be put on. (But for myself I don't believe in advertising the fact, that when anyone joins the Colours, people should make a song about it. It's only what is right.)[29] I am very glad you went home to tea yesterday; & that you cheered Ma up a bit. She will need it badly I think, for she is taking this job far too serious. Why worry at all I say. I'm quite alright. It's you at home who has the biggest task by a long way. You must call in as often as you can darling. I don't think you would do for a lady postwoman. You are far too pretty for that.[30] Have you had your photo taken yet? I should so love to have one, so as to think that although I cannot have you with me always at present, I can have the next best thing. I have not got all my kit yet, but I shall have mine taken as soon as I get my putties[31] & belt. We were re-moving yesterday into different huts, so my hut in future is No 39 instead of 43. The address is just the same excepting that. If you happen to be up Marsh to-morrow at any time, just slip in & tell Ma this, as it is rather important. You see when there are about 45 huts & 1,600 men it makes it rather awkward for me to get my letters from you; as everybody has been moved. I can just immagine Harry Heaton's face when you told him where I had gone to. What a lark! Has the R.F.A.[32] left Hudd'd yet for Morcambe? … I went to Chapel yesterday morning, & thought about you during the whole of the service. 'How nice it would be if I were with you at the Anniversary at Home,' I thought. And the old old lane too, sweetheart. But there, I must keep your spirits up mustn't it? …

I duly received your parcel & loving letter this morning, quite safely, but find that I cannot thank you or mother, enough for them. They were simply lovely. I have eaten the buns & biscuits this afternoon, but have left the cake for to-night & to-morrow. Oh! my darling, I cannot understand why you are all so good to me. It isn't as if I had done something good or great. And as for being proud of me, why, that's all tommyrot. There's nothing to be proud of sweetheart, that I can see of. I'm only trying to do my *little* bit & having to rough it in the process. The weather is still keeping very hot & my face is beginning to peel. It has gone quite red & feels very sore when I wash me. In addition I have had neuralgia in the right side of my face, since last Sat. It is getting a lot better now, but sometimes when it comes on at its worst, I could scream out with pain. I had to stand at attention on Wednesday afternoon for an hour & a half & had that cheerful companion with me all the time. In addition, I had to go to bed, with it, last night by eight o'clock & it nearly drove me mad. But don't think I'm complaining, 'Beauty.' It's all in the game. The latest rumour going round the camp, is that we are going to the Isle of Man to guard the German prisoners there.[33] (Fancy us going to guard anything above a Glow-worm.) But I think, really, that A, B, C & D Company is going to Masham on Tuesday, for rifle practice; leaving 'E' Co. here. Then, in a fortnight, we are going to Leeds for recruiting purposes, as they are talking of forming a second Battalion; & Leeds is our head-quarters. However, let's hope so. Frank Crosland got a pass home last Tuesday, but is due back to-night. I shall be seeing him to-morrow & will get to know all the home news. He said he would call & see Ma yesterday; so she will be telling you about it when you go up home again. I had a letter from Walter this morning & he tries, as usual, to be humourous. I will drop him a line or two in a day or so.

I am glad you liked the 'Palladium'[34] last Monday. I have not been to the pictures this week as I feel somewhat lost when Frank is away. I have not been out this week except as far as the 'Y.M.C.A.' Hut. As you seem to want to do something so badly for me, my child, I will set you a little task… will you try & get me a small pocket mirror? Something about six inches by three. You see there are about 30 in our hut & we've only one looking-glass to join at. So you'll see that it's very inconvenient when we all want to shave in a morning…

FROM LUCY, 18 JUNE 1915

To Henry, Hut 39, E Company, 17th West Yorkshires, Raikswood Camp.

Dear Henry,

I was so glad to receive your loving letter, oh you do send some nice ones and they do me heaps of good I simply love to have them, but I am afraid writing to me is taking up to much of your time and that's not right is it. Yet I should be disappointed if you did not write so there you are. And please dont say its good of me to send you parcels, it is nothing of the sort, it is the only way I can let you know how much I love you and think about you in these weary days of separation, and besides it is my duty & I love to do it so I dont want any thanks you see. Thank you very much for setting me a little task as you call it. I will go shopping to-morrow, and get a nice compact mirror that will fit the pocket and at the same time be useful and then I will send it on for, it certainly must be very akward for you as things are, and you know dear I broke the one you had, do you remember when you was lifting me down those steps in Greenhead Park I cracked it all to bits, so I shall only be replacing it you see. I went to see your Ma last night, and we had such a nice talk together we are firm friends now Henry dear, she told me about Frank Croslands visit and all the news

about you, in fact I was there till twenty past ten. I am sorry
to hear you have neuralgia its terrible, Mother has had it this
week and she says she can feel sorry she knows what it is, and
being away from home makes it worse. I do hope you will
soon be alright again dear, your Ma said she thought she would
go to Manchester to-night & stay until Monday she was a bit
undecided, but I told her the change would do her good, so
I think she is going. I suppose Walter Waterworth has been to
see her, and asked how she was getting on without you, he
also said he had heard from you, you dont forget anyone you
dear loving boy. You say you are only 30 miles away from me, I
know that dear but it seems such a long long [way] away, and it
seems months since you went, Oh I do long to see you again, I
want you so much. You wish me pleasant dreams but not about
you, you say. I think of you waking and sleeping so there is
no wonder I dream about you is there. I am not worrying *too*
much Henry dear you cant worry to much about some one
you love, and to be cheerful seems almost impossible, in fact
Mr Waterworth at the shop (Walter's uncle I mean you know)
calls me the Sunshine of Paradise Alley of course that's sarcasm
because I look gloomy, but I dont take any notice, they dont
understand. Oh by the way Miss Blackshaw has asked to be
remembered to you lots of times and every time I have written
yet I have forgotten to tell you, I scribble away and forget lots
of things I mean to tell you, of course thats just like me is it not
dear. I'm always doing something silly. We are going to have
another Military Display in Huddersfield before long, I have
enclosed a bill about it so you will see what I mean.[35] Well I
think it is time I gave up worrying you, dont you but will write
again soon and send glass. So now I will close.
With fondest love and kisses. I remain your loving little
Sweetheart Lu.
PS Mother sends her best love and hopes too see you soon. Lu.

Very many thanks for your sweet loving letter which I received quite safely, last Saturday morning. I am sorry that I had only time to send you a P.C. for yesterday but there was a Concert in the 'Y.M.' room on Saturday night & they cleared all the tables etc away. It was a very mild affair. Boy Scouts & Girl Guides. Songs & dances etc. Just like a Band of Hope Prize Giving at Gledholt.[36] You know the kind of thing I mean. 'Summer Fairies;' only I do it better. We stuck it until eight o'clock & then we were simply fed up & had to go. Yesterday was a red letter day for your humble. Went to Chapel twice. Once compulsory & once voluntary. It was the Anniversary you see. Please make a note of it darling, it might never happen again. I had a parcel & letter from Ma on Saturday morning, containing more grub etc. & she tells me about your going up home[37] on Thursday evening & staying until after ten o'clock. It is so good of you to devote some of your spare time in visiting her & I cannot thank you enough. You see she is so lonely my darling. We have been having Rifle Drill to-day for the first time, & have felt very awkward with them, but I think we shall improve. When we have all our pack on; including rifle & overcoat, we carry over 90 pounds. Not a bad little weight to go on a ten or fifteen mile march with, is it beauty? I have had a letter from Teddy & Willie this morning, but they say nothing new. I am enclosing you a cutting from the 'Yorkshire Post,' referring to an accident, which I think will interest you. Lieu. Roscoe was the officer of 'E' Co, and a very decent fellow indeed. He is very very badly injured, they say here that he is almost on the point of dying. However, let's hope he will recover.[38] Companys A, B, C & D leave here to-morrow (Tuesday) for Masham, but 'E' Co remains behind. I think we are booked for Leeds for a recruiting campaign, as they are thinking of forming another Battalion. But more of that when I get to know definate. I hope it's true sweetheart. I might be able to get home at week-ends then. I had an 'Examiner' from Ma the other day & was sorry to read of young Fletchers's accident in the 'R.F.A.' I hope its nothing very serious. We are very lucky here, as there has been no accidents, bar a sprained ankle or two. But the most exciting time is when some of the men come in drunk. We had one the other night who came in fresh & then had a fit. It took eight men to hold him down. Then we had another who came in drunk, quarrelled with some of the men, & then threw a bucket of hot coffee over them. Quite exciting I assure you. Ten days 'B.C.' [sic – C.B.] Which means they are confined to Barracks for ten days, with an hours pack drill each evening. Frank is going along with 'C' Company to-morrow to Masham, so I shall feel lonelier than ever…

FROM HENRY, RAIKSWOOD CAMP, 22 JUNE 1915

Just a little note to thank you so much for the lovely pocket-mirror, which you so kindly sent to me, & which I received safely this morning. It is very good of you sweetheart, & besides being a little keepsake, is just the thing I wanted in these hard times of poverty & starvation. (Edison Bell Record.)[39] You will, no doubt, have received my brain-fagger by this time & will have digested it by now; but I simply couldn't resist another letter to-night… I shall try & get a pass home in a fortnight or so, but I have been wondering if father could bring you over in the Car some Sunday on one of his trips out to Harrogate or Ilkley.[40] They allow visitors in the camp grounds on Saturdays & Sundays but they are prohibited in the huts. Please do not think me cheeky or forward in suggesting this; but I am dying to see you & kiss you again 'beauty.' So if it could not be managed, please do not think anything more of it. You could have tea here & then father could call for you on his return journey. However, try your best darling & let

me know how you get on. The four Companys left here for
Masham this afternoon & we cheered them off. I am glad to
hear that Bertie Sheard is still in the land of the living & that he
is still busy collecting money. I must write to him before long
& a host of other people, including Luke. I knew that I had a
piece of news to tell you, but quite forgot it until now. That's
the worst of these cheap brains. They're so unreliable. But there
has come to sleep in the next bed to me, a young fellow from
Aspley[41] named Dawson. We had quite a long chat the other
night when I got to know he came from Huddersfield. He
worked at Brown & Thomas,[42] Painters, High St. before he
enlisted, knows Miss Noel, & is a friend of the Artist's. Also,
he used to live at Marsh & knows Willie's plain May & all
the family. In addition he knows 'Burnham;' but that's scarcely
worth mentioning, as we're writing about gentlemen. Happily
(& no wonder) he has the same opinion of him as I have, so we
shan't fall out over that…

Arm-bands used by charity collectors in the Huddersfield area 1915–16. Lucy mentioned
Rose Day, War Horse Day and Poland's Day in her letters. (Kirklees Museums collection)

FROM HENRY, RAIKSWOOD CAMP, 24 JUNE 1915

…I stayed in the 'Y.M.' last night, reading, until about nine o'clock, & then I went back to the 'Little Grey Home in the West.' (That's No. 39 in Skipton dialect.) This morning we were up at 5-30, paraded at 6-30 & went for a three mile march before breakfast. It was lovely out, first thing, but it has turned dreadfully cold since. The men are all wearing their great-coats to-night, & it has been trying to rain all day, but has not succeeded up to now. This afternoon we have been having more rifle exercise in a field corner & skirmishing behind hedges. Quite exciting I assure you. I cannot get a pass home this week-end, but will try very hard for one for the week-end after; but I will let you know when I get it. I am sorry to hear that young Fletcher is so bad, but hope he'll pull through. I'm rather surprised at the Authorities allowing them to have such a horse, after the other two mishaps with it, but I suppose they think anything will do for the Army…

PS You might send me an 'Examiner,' darling.

FROM HENRY, RAIKSWOOD CAMP, 29 JUNE 1915

I was glad to receive your loving cheerful letter this morning & thank you for it. I duly received the 'Examiner' you sent me, last Sat. night, & have read it through & passed it on to a Holmfirth man who I have found lives in our hut. I hope you had a good sale of Roses last Sat. but wasn't it a beastly day? It rained here nearly all the day. Evidently they hadn't all the pretty darlings out selling Roses, as I heard you were working. (That's a delicate compliment for you.) Well, I'll begin by telling you my doings of the last few days, as I know you like to hear them. On Saturday, I did not turn out further than the 'Y.M.' as my heels were very bad. I had to go on 'sick' with them last Friday & see the doctor. He said 'Stay in & rest them & don't come on

morning. Also to thank you for your sweet love-letter which you enclosed. We have been a route march to-day to a place called Thornton (but I believed I mentioned it yesterday in my letter to you) which is about five miles away from here; but we went about 15 miles in all, as we took a circular route there & back. We have had our full pack on, including overcoat, but have not carried rifles; but it has been quite sufficient without. It is about 86 lbs in all, so I don't think we have done so bad, do you sweetheart? We had no early morning parade, but paraded at 9 o'clock & started at 9-30 in the pouring rain. It did not rain long, however, & the sun came out & it was glorious. We arrived at Thornton alright & the whole inhabitants (about 30) turned out to meet us & gave us a good reception. It is only quite a small place, but is right in the heart of the Country. We had our dinner there at 1 o'clock (just about the time you would be having yours darling) & we all sat down in a field. Bread & Butter & Corned Beef was the 'menu;' washed down by water from our water bottles. Tell Ma that I had the pasty you sent me, for 'desert,' & it tasted lovely. We started on the road again at a quarter to two; after having had a wash in a horse trough; & had a good send off by the villagers; & arrived back at the Camp again about five o'clock: tired & hungry. I am feeling well & tired & healthy & nearly happy, as I write this to you sweetheart; but I cannot feel perfectly happy without you, my beloved. We had three men who fell out on the march; so I think I did very well to stick it. They fainted away & dropped down in the road just like a stone. We took them to the side of the road & laid them on the grass, & left a man to watch them. He stopped the first motor-car that came along, & it brought them back to Skipton. But the whole Company never stopped; it still marched on… You would laugh at our boys as they are on the March. When they pass a farm-house they sing 'For to be a farmer's boy' & when they pass a pretty dear they sing 'If it's a Lady, Thumbs up.' Well I really must come to a conclusion as I think this is about all at present; until I hear from you again. I have not heard from Ma this week yet, but perhaps I shall get a letter in the morning. So goodnight my darling & pleasant dreams. Give my love to Mother & kind regards to father & the Boys.

FROM HENRY, RAIKSWOOD CAMP, 18 JULY 1915

Very many thanks for your long loving letter which I received alright yesterday. You must forgive me for not replying last night (& I know you will have been horribly disappointed at not receiving a letter this morning) but I went to the Skipton Hospital Gala & did not get back until late. We had an extension until eleven o'clock, so we could stay & see the Fireworks, & in honour of the event I suppose. I had a very good time on the whole, but missed my darling sweetheart, as usual. It felt quite like old times being out when the shops are lighted up. We had to go on Parade at 2 o'clock & take part in the Procession; & we led the way, the 'Boy Scouts' following. It was just like our Whit Tuesday procession[45] & the Gala was held in a field, by the Castle… I forgot to mention that there was a tug-of-war, at the Gala, between our chaps & some of the 6th West Ridings (Territorials)[46], but they just beat us…

FROM HENRY, RAIKSWOOD CAMP, 19 JULY 1915

Just a few lines to say I received your usual loving letter this morning & thank you ever so much for it. I am glad that you liked your little present, sweetheart, & that the Hat-Pins suit; but you mustn't talk about the money they cost & what I spend on you my darling. That is of no consequence whatever & it is just a very wee bit in repayment for what you & Mother have done for me since I came to Skipton. Think of the lovely parcel that comes every week… Oh Lucy darling, you are a girl in a thousand & I am perfectly certain that there never was a luckier mortal than I am. I have all your true love for myself & the knowledge that you are for ever thinking of me. Also that some day (in the near future I hope) I shall have the happiness of having you all to myself & will be able to hold you in my arms & kiss you whenever I like. Could anyone wish for anything lovelier than that my beauty? And now, my darling, I have a bit of fresh news to tell you. We are leaving here (after many false alarms) for Colsterdale (nr. Ripon) on Saturday next. This is certain, for the Captain told us all, this morning & he said he had heard definate from the War-Office, yesterday. We shall leave Skipton sometime in the afternoon, & are going into Huts again; but he does not seem to think that we shall stay there long. So don't post anything for me after Friday evening until I send you my new address; which I will do as soon as I can… They have taken all our Rifles away from here, & we are going to have new Service Rifles[47] when we get to Colsterdale. Ready for India or France or any old place I suppose…

FROM HENRY, RAIKSWOOD CAMP, 22 JULY 1915

Very many thanks for another of your sweet letters which I received quite safely this morning. I am on Sentry Guard again darling & am writing this to you about one o'clock in the morning. A nice time to be writing love letters isn't it my beauty? But then you see this is about the only chance I shall get to-day & I don't want to disappoint you of your letter, if I can possibly help it 'beauty.' I came on guard at 6 o'clock yesterday until 6 o'clock to-night & have just done my first spell of duty: 10 o'clock until 12, so I am at liberty to write to you until four if I can find enough paper to fill. It is as dark as pitch outside & raining heavily, & I have been thinking of you sweetheart, as I paced my lonely verandah. If anyone had told us, six months ago, that 'your humble' would 'come down' to guarding a verandah with a fixed bayonet; we should have been inclined to laugh & murmah 'Stores-Hall.'[48] But here the fact remains. We have started to clear up for our departure on Saturday & have given over drilling for the present. Our advance party, consisting of 40 men & one officer, left here for Coldersdale at 9 o'clock this morning, so they should be there by now. The Bradford Territorials[49] are coming here on Sat. for a time, and their advance party came at noon to-day. They are a fine lot of men, but they have been billeted at home up to the present, so it looks like breaking a few of their hearts, coming to live in huts. However, 'if you broke your Mother's heart you won't break mine. About turn.' And now my darling I will answer a few things in your letter. In the first place, it isn't a 'tax on my time' to write to you so often, but a labour of love my sweetheart. I love to write to you & to have your sweet loving letters in reply. I am glad you think me your hero beauty, because I want to be that; but for myself I think I'm more like the 'Chocolate Soldier,'[50] never minding the 'Hero.' However, you shall have it your own way darling. My Neuralgia is a little better but not much. I went to see the doctor yesterday morning; & he said 'Medicine & Duty.' I was that disgusted that I came away. I have done the 'duty,' but have not seen anything of the medicine yet. It will be coming about August Bank Holiday I suppose; but when it does come it will go down the drain. I can doctor myself better. I read in the 'Leeds Mercury' about the explosion at Leitch's Chemical Works & it must have been awful.[51] …

FROM LUCY, 23 JULY 1915

Thank you so very much for the loving letter you sent which I received last night (Thursday). I had had a miserable day at the shop, and oh Henry dear how welcome your letter was, I forget everything else when I read them, but really dear you ought not to write to me when you should be resting. And I am sure you must be tired after two hours on guard. I hate to think of you being on guard dear, it seems so terrible watching and waiting all through the long night. And then having to sleep on the boards, oh my darling boy my heart aches for you. I had not gone to bed dear when you was writing my letter but was sat at my bedroom window looking out into the rain & darkness and thinking of you, for it rained heavily here, and I thought Henry will be in bed but it seems I was mistaken. Oh if only I could have been with you through the lonely hours how happy I should have been, but such things cannot be can they Henry darling. I expect by now you will have got the letter I sent on Wednesday. I went to see your Ma last night and she told me she had written too, of course as usual I stayed quite late, and oh my darling boy everything up at home reminds me of you, and the happy times you and I have spent there. I met Willie yesterday dinner-time and he told me that Frank was coming over to-day (Friday) and I think I saw him tonight as I was coming home from the shop but I wont be sure. Willie also said something about Franks company going to Leeds. I think Gladys will come over next Tuesday because it is Willie's Birthday he wants her to at any rate. I was sorry to hear of your Neuralgia troubling you again, and as for the wretched doctor I would just like to tell him what I think about him nasty old thing. When I said you was a bad boy Henry dear I only meant it in fun you know that dont you dear you are all the world to me and I love you ever so much and I would never love any one that was bad, it was because I knew that you was noble, and honourable, and generous, that I first loved you, and my opinion will never change so there my sweetheart. I do hope dear you will have a nice day for moving to-morrow it will be awful if the weather is bad, & I shall be quite anxious to hear from you to know how you have got on. Will you let me know dear how far you are from a station, and which is the nearest, that is as soon as you get to know because I do want to come and see you as soon as I can. You say I am sweet & loving dear, but how could I be otherwise than loving, when you give me such love in return, and I am glad I mean so much to you in your loneliness, if only I was worth half the love you shower upon me I would not mind, *but* dear my love for you is at least true & good I could never be false to you, and as long as you want me I am yours. Thank you ever so much for the Cards you sent the boys you have just made the set up of 'Overseas'[52] for them and they both thank you very much. Mr Waterworth at the shop, asked me this morning if it was a dark night when you met me, he says he is sure you will have to close your eyes every time you kiss me, my face is so awful of course I dont take any notice of him, and I told him that if it was anything like his I would pawn it, so I think I got my own back dont you dear. Well dear I dont think I have much more news, so I will close I think I have troubled you long enough. So goodnight my dear loving boy, and may God watch over you & keep you safe that is the earnest prayer of your loving and trusting sweetheart.

Lu.

PS Mother sends her love, she is very sorry about your Neuralgia she has had it all week. Will you please excuse pencil dear but my pen is such a scratchy old thing. Leah at Elland told father she had had a letter from you on Wed. Lu.

FROM HENRY, RAIKSWOOD CAMP, 23 JULY 1915

Just a few lines to thank you for the lovely cakes & biscuits which you sent me; not forgetting the sweet love-letter. I cannot thank you enough sweetheart, so I am not going to try, but it is there all the time & you understand perfectly, my own. I think this is about the last time I shall write to you from here dear, for we leave for Colsterdale at 3-45 to-morrow. We should arrive at Masham about 10 o'clock & then we have another 6 miles to march to Colsterdale; so we look like landing there in the wee small hours of Sunday morning. (Colsterdale does not possess a Railway Station of it's own, you see sweetheart, so Masham happens to be the nearest.) I suppose the Authorities put it there for (in)-convenience & just to show there was no ill-feeling. What a pic-nic we are going to have & especially if it rains. But this blessed life is full of 'pic-nics,' or else *I'll* resign. And talking of pic-nics we've another one coming to-night. They have packed all the bed-steads & straw mattresses & pillows away for removal; so we shall have to sleep on the floor again with our overcoats for pillows. Still I am getting quite used to sleeping anywhere & anyhow, & could sleep on a clothes line if they'd only peg me on securely. However its all in a life-time so I mustn't complain my darling. I had a parcel from Ma by the same post so I am well up for grub at present. I am taking some with me to Colsterdale, as I expect we shall be short for a day or two, & I refuse to live on fresh air & grass & so fade away into 'nothingness.' It isn't worth it, is it darling? Your parcel came whilst I was on guard, so I could not get to open it until I came off at 6 o'clock last night. Tell Mother that I am not going to be made into a Farmer's Boy. I am a 'City Clerk' by profession & a 'Boy Scout' (at present) by occupation. And the old women, I refuse to talk to, as I suppose they will only be able to talk about 'Lloyd George' & 'old age pensions;' but I am nearly ready for mine now so I had better shut up. I smiled when I read in your letter about the 'Hudd.' Territorials[53] & their fixed bayonets. They should be on guard over here, at the bottom of the wood, when you see 'Ghosts' & owls etc.; all through the night, & have no one to talk to except the rats. I think they'd want some 'Wrigley's Spearmint' then, my beauty. Just to cheer them up & help them on their way. Still it isn't their fault, sweetheart, they are only trying to do their bit just like we fellows over here...

Colsterdale is in the Ure valley, about five miles from Masham. Leeds City Council owned the land, and set it aside for a camp for the Leeds Pals (15th Bn West Yorkshire regiment) in September 1914. The camp was completed in October. In June the 15th Battalion moved to Ripon to form part of the 93rd Brigade, and the camp became a training area for the reserve companies of the 15th and 17th Battalions, which were designated the 19th Reserve Bn West Yorkshire Regiment. Other reserve companies joined them – hence Henry's bewildered comment about the variety of regiments. Eventually the camp consisted of numerous huts, an orderly room, canteen, guardroom, sergeants' mess, dining hall, ablutions, bath-houses and parade ground. However when Henry was stationed there most troops were apparently still housed in tents. The site remains open land today, and the locations of the buildings are visible as earthworks. There is also a monument to the Leeds Pals.[54]

FROM HENRY, COLSTERDALE CAMP, MASHAM, 25 JULY 1915

Many thanks for another of your loving letters which I received alright yesterday morning. Well darling, we arrived here late last night & it is a hole & no error. As one of our fellows said, 'It's the last place God made, & he sent the Bantams here to finish it.' We are under canvas not in huts as expected & there are 15,000 of soldiers here within a radius of twelve miles. There are Companys of the Leeds Pals, Bradford Pals, Northumberland Fusileers, Birkenhead Bantams & goodness knows who else. There are ten of us in a tent & so I have christened ours the 'Ten Lunies.' Very appropriate isn't it? Well, to return to our journey yesterday. We left Skipton at our stated time & said goodbye to all its inhabitants. We got as far as Leeds, got shunted on to the Gt. Eastern Railway & then

Postcard of Gladys Cooper. Henry sent Lucy many postcards of this type. (Private collection)

rightaway for this hole. We came through Harrogate, Ripon & on to Masham. Masham is about 40 miles off Leeds & is a dead end. That is, the end of the line & I am told that there was only one train a week until we came here. We arrived at Masham about 8 o'clock & then was given an hours rest until 9. And then the fun began. We set off to tramp to this place which is about 6 miles further on & arrived at about 11 o'clock, just about dead tired. Then we found there was no tents up & no blankets had arrived. So I rolled myself up in my great coat & went to sleep in a field corner. Just to get a bit of fresh air you know sweetheart. It's good for the complexion. However we've got the tents up this morning (Sunday) & started to sort ourselves out a bit. There is a light railway runs down to

Masham from here, but it only goes once a day. We have to
have our post ready by 4–30 or else it doesn't go until next day.
We wash ourselves in buckets & have our meals in our Mess-
Tins.[55] There is not a house in sight & two miles to go to the
nearest village. What a pic-nic! There is about three Canteens,
half a dozen shops & also a fire-station. The only part about it
is the scenary which is lovely. You can see nothing but fields &
moors for miles away. Well I shall have to knock of now darling
as I am writing this on a dinner-plate & they want it for dinner.
Write back sweetheart as soon as you can.

FROM LUCY, 26 JULY 1915

Thank you very much for your letters, both the one I recieved
this morning and the one I got on Saturday. I thought about
you on Saturday night and all day on Sunday wondering
how you were going on and if you had arrived safe. Oh I was
shocked when I knew you had slept in a field corner how
awful it was for you dear. I saw your Ma in the park on Sunday
afternoon and had a nice talk to her, and at night after Chapel
I went home with her & stayed supper, we did have a nice
time oh my sweetheart how I wish you had been with us, your
pussy jumped up on my knee and went to sleep there and
every time your Ma put him down he came back again, so you
see what good friends we are. I am sorry dear you have got
to such a miserable place how lonely you will be my darling
boy I do hope you wont have to stay there long. Do you think
it is possible for me to come over for the day dear. I should
like to so much and I dont care whether I walk six miles or
sixty if only I can see you for the day. will you please let me
know what you think dear. Your Ma says the little boys from
Manchester are coming to-morrow (Tuesday) to stay with her
for a time so she will not be quite so lonely dear now will
she. There has been quite a lot of the R.F.A. boys over from

Ripon this week and they have only been away a fort-night, Laurence the Tram man being one of them. How I wish you were coming over again Henry dear. I do want to see you again and feel your loving arms about me again. I miss you my sweetheart more than words can tell what a glad time it will be for me when you come home for good never to leave me again, but there I must be patient, and hope for the best though I find it a very difficult thing to do my darling boy. Will you give my kind regards to the Holmfirth gentleman & thank him for enquiring about me. I note what you say about Gladys Cooper,[56] oh you are a treat Henry just as full of fun as ever. I dont think you will ever be anything but jolly you dear boy. Well I dont think I have anything more to say only that I hope things will improve for you quickly and that you will have as nice a time as possible during your stay at Ripon. So now I will close with love from all at home.

Yours for Ever & Ever Lu.

PS What would I not give for a kiss just now dear. Lu.

FROM HENRY, COLSTERDALE CAMP, 27 JULY 1915

…I have had a good look around the Camp & it is bigger than I thought it was at first. It is just like the South Shore at Blackpool, with its wooden shops, miniature railway & sandy & pebbly roads. You say in your last letter that you would like to come & see me over here; but for goodness sake don't darling. You would never get back. It is 6 miles tramp to Masham & over a road similar to that, that runs from Outlane to the Junction at Oldham. I am going to put in for a pass for next week-end, but it will be all travelling there & back I think. Still it will be worth it just to see your sweet face my darling & to hold you in my arms & cover you with kisses. The Camp makes its own Electric Light & is also on the Trunk Telephone, so don't be surprised if I ring you up one of these days, although I am

nearly 60 miles away. You can tell Mr Waterworth from me
that it wasn't a dark night when I met you (it was a Wednesday
afternoon wasn't it sweetheart) & besides if it had of been I
should have been quite satisfied. Dark nights are better than
moon-light ones to cuddle & kiss you on my sweetheart. But I
might have forgotten how to do that by the next time I see you
again. What do you say darling? (Not likely.) I have just seen
three women since I came here last Saturday up to to-night
(Tuesday) so you can tell what sort of a hole it is. We seem to
be miles from civilization… We get our water from a spring &
it is perfectly clean & fresh, but we have to wash ourselves in
buckets. Oh! for the simple life. (I *don't* think.)…

FROM HENRY, COLSTERDALE CAMP, 28 JULY 1915

Very many thanks for your long loving letter which I have
received at last… Well darling, I don't know that there is
anything fresh to tell you, except that I am still living the
'Gipsy' life. We went for a six mile route march this afternoon
(with our full packs on) & went over some of the most awful
roads & hills I have been over since I started 'Boy Scouting;' &
I have been over a few during my two months service. Roads
as hard as granite, hills as big as hill 60[57] & through streams &
small rivers in galore. However its part of the training my child.
You say in your letter that you would like to come over for the
day sometime. My darling, by the time you got here, the day
would be over, & you would want another one to get back in. I
am sorry sweetheart, but although I am dying to see your sweet
face again & to kiss all your troubles away, I cannot let you
come here, as you are far too precious to me to be lost in this
dreary wilderness, miles from civilization. The only way you
can manage it is by motor, so you had better see what Father
says. I am glad you went home with Ma last Sunday night
after Chapel, & that you looked after our Dreadnought for me.

Female tram conductor. The smart uniforms were much remarked on, although many men were bemused that women could carry out such jobs traditionally reserved for men. (Kirklees Image Archive km03737)

There is a small chapel at the bottom of our parade ground, but the nearest Church is three miles away. You say in your letter, darling, that you hope our stay at Ripon will be pleasant. But my sweet little Girl, we are 16 miles from Ripon. I wish we was at Ripon. It would be better than this place which is worse than the Alps…

The huge numbers of men flocking to the armed forces created vacancies in many works, which led to unprecedented opportunities for women to enter the workplace. On 28 July 1915 the Huddersfield Examiner *carried a story headed 'Women Tram Conductors: Great Interest in Huddersfield's latest innovation.' Like Henry and Lucy, the reporter displayed an amused condescension at the situation: 'Something of the nature of a mild sensation was caused among passengers travelling on the Lockwood and Fartown cars yesterday afternoon, for they discovered four attractive young ladies learning* the duty of tram conducting. The ladies seemed very businesslike, for they wore the customary cross-over belts with bell-punch and cash-bag. As to their enthusiasm and zeal it was obvious to anyone who watched them quickly learning the duties the old adage "None but the brave deserve the fair" will have to be altered to "None but the fair deserve the fare."

FROM LUCY, 29 JULY 1915

Thank you very much for your very welcome letter which I received just as I was going to work this morning. I see that up to the time of writing you had not got my letter, though I wrote and posted it on Monday night, but it was raining so I did not go to the General so perhaps that was the reason of the delay, as the collections from the boxes are very uncertain. I feel very sorry for you dear, you have got to a wretched place and no mistake. You seem to be going from bad to worse, Skipton was a bit nearer civilization wasn't it dear, I am awfully sorry about your neuralgia too you have quite enough to put up with without that I know. And then being under canvas wont be like huts, I suppose & you will get wet through when it rains, oh it is dreadful and I feel quite miserable when I think about it all and then you say you are not brave, but I know different, and I admire and love you more than ever if that is possible dear. I am very sorry that I can't come over to see you I did want to come, and intended coming August Bank Holiday Monday, still you know best dear and if you think it unwise, I will give up all thoughts of it, and try and wait until you can come over, I do hope you will get a pass when you put in dear for oh I am dying to see you, it seems ages since you went back and I have been lonely and sad ever since, the days coming and going unheeded Oh but it is time I gave up talking in this strain it does not sound very brave does it dear, and now for a bit of news that will amuse you I know, we have got some lady conductors dear just like you said we

should have, but at present they are only on the Honley & Sheepbridge [Sheepridge] section, I suppose they are on trial. I know you will pity the drivers wont you? but Marion and I are thinking of applying do you think we would do I am afraid we should very soon get into difficulties. Phylis has had a card from Arnold Newsome and he is at South Camp Ripon wherever that might be.[58] Fancy having Trunk Telephone service in the Camp dear, I should love you to ring me up at our Office it would seem quite like old times wouldn't it dear. We had a War horse day here on Saturday and raised £1000, not bad was it, instead of flags little horse shoes were sold with a horses head in the centre.[59] I am sending a small parcel also an Examiner with the usual local news. Harry Watson is on his holidays so Marion is downhearted this week, he has told her that if she is *very* good he *might* send her a postcard, what do you think about that? I'm afraid I should have told him not to bother at all. We are Stocktaking at the Shop this week and we shall close on Thursday from 2 to 5 while the committee men are at work, it has caused us all a lot of extra work this week and really I have not felt equal to it, in fact I have not been myself for a bit now, there are times when I feel properly ill, but then we have been very busy lately perhaps that has something to do with it, and you see I miss your love and kisses and sweet sympathy so much dear, there is no one to tell all my troubles to now and no one to spoil me, and kiss me and make me forget everything except one loving presence like you used to do, but never mind you will be back some day and then everything else will be forgotten. Well dear I dont think I have much more news so I will close with fondest love and kisses I remain
Yours Lovingly & forever Lu.
PS Father says he feels sorry for you he knows what sort of a place you have got to, he would be pleased to hear from you any time you care to write. Mother sends her best love and

hopes your Neuralgia will soon be better. The boys wish to be remembered. Lu.

FROM LUCY, 30 JULY 1915

Thank you very much for your letter which came at half past five yesterday (Thursday) I see that at the time of writing you had not got the letter and parcel I sent on Wednesday, but of course I put near Masham on so perhaps that would delay it, I went to see Ma last night and she said she sent you a small parcel of medicine on Wednesday and put Masham on, so we both hope you have got them safe and shall know in future to leave the word out altogether. I am very sorry that my first letter was so long in reaching you, you would think I had forgotten you, it seems such a long time from Saturday to Wednesday without a letter does it not Henry dear, I know that if I dont hear from you for a day or two I get downhearted and I expect you will be the same. I should think it will be very awkward for you having to have the letters ready for post by 4-30 it does not give you much time. I was very sorry to hear of your Neuralgia being so bad, and trust that by now it will be better, at any rate I think the stuff your Ma sent should do you good, I do hope so. It seems awful for me to be here and helpless while you are going through so much, here I am unable to do anything for you, when if I could I would do so much, instead I have to stay here and love you, but I do that dear with all my heart, and always shall you know that dont you my darling boy. I did not think you was so far out of Ripon dear I was surprised when you said 16 miles. Thank you very much for your assurances of love Henry dear, they are very sweet to me my own boy, and make me feel all the stronger for the task of waiting & longing for your speedy return. Thank you very much for the cards you enclosed for the boys, it is good of you to think about them. The little boys from Manchester have not come, and your Ma was disappointed but she thinks they will come at the weekend. The lady train guards are to have a uniform with a high military collar so wont they be fine but judging from the talk of the drivers they dont like the idea at all, so these charming young ladies look like having a rough time what do you think? Well dear I dont think I have much more news. Only I do hope you wont be long before you get a pass I want to see you so very much I feel so sad & lonely without you my sweetheart, I had got to look upon you as part of my life, the best, and happiest part, and without you my loved one it is a hopeless blank. The old lane is just the same as ever sweetheart, though I dont venture down very often, it is more than I can stand, you know why dont you my sweetheart, but there I must stop, so with fondest love & heaps of kisses,

I remain, yours now and forever, Lu.

PS The big kiss at the bottom dear is for luck. Lu.

FROM HENRY, COLSTERDALE CAMP, 30 JULY 1915

Very many thanks for another of your loving letters & also the parcel, which I received quite safely last night. I am sorry to say however, that the contents of the parcel were broken up into little bits & the box was squashed always. But it was as welcome as the flowers in May, & I really can't thank you & Mother enough for it, my sweetheart. When I think about you all at home, my beloved, it makes a lump come into my throat & its hard work sometimes to keep back the tears. Oh, my darling, we thought it was bad at Skipton but it is a thousand times worse here. Skipton was a palace compared with this. Our fellows are deserting by the dozen. It has been very hot during the last few days & there are thousands of flies about the place. A lot of the fellows are down with sickness & I shouldn't wonder if there was fever next. Many thanks for the 'Examiner,' darling, before I forget it. I read it through last night. I had a small parcel of medicine this morning from Ma & a box of grub to-night. Did you go up home as usual last night sweetheart? I hope you did as I thought about you all the night. I went to see the Doctor this morning & he gave me three days rest. My feet are very sore again & my face is all puffed up owing to having constant Neuralgia. I do look a 'guy' darling & no mistake. What a pic-nic! I could stick it until further orders if I could only keep well. But all my luck is out since I came here. If Arnold Newsome, at South Camp, Ripon, is anything like we are here, he'll wish he'd never left their Emily. It will break his heart. The grub we get is not so very bad, but it could be improved by a long way. We can't keep the grass out of it & I have eaten enough grass since I came here, to keep a little horse for a week. We are having holiday on Monday for Bank Holiday but it's not much good that I can see of. There's nothing to do. I hope you will have a good time. I am rather interested in the Lady Conductor & smiled to myself when I read it. 'Fares ready please & mind my powder puff.' But I don't think you'd do for a Conductor sweetheart. There's enough with me going through the 'mill' at present, without you starting sweetheart…

FROM HENRY, COLSTERDALE CAMP 1 AUGUST 1915

Just a few lines once more, to tell you that I am still existing. It is Sunday evening as I write this, just about 6 o'clock & is pouring with rain. You will just about be getting ready for Chapel, won't you sweetheart? The rain is coming in our tent in a steady stream, so we shall have to start 'bailing' out I suppose before long. One of our fellows has just found out that the rain is coming in, & that we are having a 'stream' of it, so the Corporal in charge said:- 'Well don't report it or they'll all want one.' We had a 'drum-head' service this morning, but it only lasted half an hour & was not impressive. This afternoon I went with a

The Old Soldier never dies,
Neither does the (K)nut.

A 'Knut' or smart young man. In this cartoon, drawn by a patient at Huddersfield War Hospital, the wounded knut wears 'hospital blues.'
(Huddersfield War Hospital Magazine 1917)

few more fellows for a walk & got lost. We went for about eight miles & did not get back until about 5-30. To-night it looks like stoping in if it does not clear up. It is miserable enough here when it is fine, but fifty times worse when it rains. We have a day's holiday to-morrow, in honour of Bank Holiday I suppose, so I think I shall go down to Masham to see Frank, if it is fine. I hope you will have a nice Bank Holiday & that it is fine for you. If you go to the Palace, just think of me my darling. I wish I could go with you, but that can't be, can it sweetheart? I wrote to Luke this morning, so he will be telling you when you go up to

Elland again. I do not know that there is anything else this time my darling, but try & keep a stout heart & don't worry yourself ill. Goodnight my sweetheart & God bless you.

FROM HENRY, COLSTERDALE CAMP 7 AUGUST 1915

…I do not know that I have any fresh news to tell you, except that it has relapsed into the old state of weather. Rain, rain & more rain & Saturday afternoon too. It is about 2 o'clock as I write this. I wonder what you are doing now my darling, serving crabby old customers with boots & shoes I suppose. I looked out for a letter from you this morning, but was disappointed. However, perhaps I shall get one in the morning. I was going down to Masham again this afternoon, but the rain is coming steadily down so I don't think I shall bother now. It is miserable here when it rains. I do not see much of young Howard now, as he is in a tent a line or two away from mine. I was talking to him last night, though & he told me he had put in for a pass but had not got one. We have our pillows & mattresses (filled with straw) back again, so it is not quite as bad as sleeping on the ground. We have been sleeping in our clothes nearly every night since we came here, so it feels quite a treat to get them off. We never know when we are going to be flooded out during the night you see. Did you go up home last Thursday night? I hope you went to stay a bit as usual. I do not know when we are leaving this hole, but I wish it was to-morrow. I am just about fed up here. No Pictures, no Palace, nobody fresh to talk to, nowhere to go to, & last but most important, I miss you, my darling, more & more every day…

FROM LUCY, 7 AUGUST 1915

Thank you very much for the letter you sent which I recieved yesterday morning it was a beautiful letter & I thank you very much for it, also for the card which I got this morning, but oh dear Henry I was disappointed I did want to see you. it was a very forlorn little girl that came to the shop this morning, but I shall have to make the best of it and look forward to your visit next week but somehow I thought you would come this week hence the great disappointment. Forgive me dear for not writing you last night as usual but father came home early and insisted on me going to the Palace with him & mother. it is a fair week and I enjoyed it but I do wish you had been with me I always do. The cigarettes enclosed[60] are from father he said he thought they would come in Handy for you but he asked me to send them for him because he has not time to write, you understand how busy he is don't you dear. Excuse pencil but I am writing this at the shop because I did want you to get it in the morning. I am using Miss Blackshaws pencil and she asks to be remembered to you, she will be away when you come next week. I went up home on Thursday to see Ma. She was hoping you would come this weekend and so were the little boys. So I am not the only disappointed one am I dear, and it is raining here to-day so perhaps next week you will have better weather I hope so. The picture postcard you sent reached me on Thursday morning it was very nice you Knut[61] What will you send next I wonder, oh and mother thanks you for hers another treat. But now I must stop we are getting busy, so keep smiling Henry dear & better luck next week with fondest love & kisses I remain Yours lovingly For Ever Lu.

FROM LUCY, 9 AUGUST 1915

Thank you very much for your loving welcome letter which I recieved this morning it was a lovely letter my sweetheart, and I thank you very much for it. I must not forget to thank you also for the one I got yesterday morning, it is good of you dear to write to me so often. I intended writing you last night after chapel, but I went to see your Ma and of course stayed so dear you must forgive me, and oh we did have a time I romped and played with the little boys, and Ma was nearly convulsed with laughing. They are dear little things though, we had Bert acting Charles Chaplin and he was a treat what a time they will have if you get over this weekend, and they do want to see you bless them. When they went to bed tired out I kissed them Goodnight and when they got upstairs Bert said Do you like that lady Freddie I do. Father thanks you very much for his letter he was pleased to hear from you dear, and will write to you when he gets the chance. Oh Henry I am sorry for you, your letter this morning made me cry, I hate to think of you suffering so because that's what you are doing and nothing less. But my darling boy for my sake don't say you want to go into the trenches, whatever should I do sweetheart if anything happened to you, I can tell you I should have no desire to live, it is only the hope that one day we shall be together again that keeps me going but I certainly do wish you could get away from Colsterdale with all its attendant evils. I do hope you get a pass this time my darling boy I want to see you so, and to feel once more your loving arms about me and forget everything in the joy of your warm soft kisses, but we shall have to trust to luck again I suppose. I am sorry you have such wretched sleeping accomodation I think it's a proper shame, how can you be expected to work without sleep. I often think about you when I go to bed at one & two in a morning & wonder whether you are asleep, or laid awake thinking of home. You say I am a girl in a thousand. Henry dear I am nothing of the sort I am only doing what any girl would do who really loved her sweetheart, and I do love you Henry dear with all my heart, and I always shall, so it affords me the greatest pleasure to write to you & keep faithful, I simply could not bear any one else after you my may I say it Henry? my husband to be, how

I love to think of that, but there all my thoughts are running away with me, that's what they do when I think of you. We had a flag day for Poland on Saturday and I understand it is the last one we are to have.[62] I saw Teddy and Willie in the Park yesterday but they did not see me for a wonder. Well dear after all this time I have had my photograph taken but they will not be ready for a week it's a wonder I did not break the Camera, but I guess I shall look like a Gollywog ready for winding up. I felt just like that, still I will see how they turn out & send you one to see what you think about them when I get them but I do hope you wont get a shock. Well dear I don't think I have any more news this time, so Goodnight & God bless you my darling soldier boy so with *fondest* love & kisses I remain Yours for Ever

Lu. [long row of kisses]

P S Thank you for the Cigarette cards dear, and do you think I dare kiss you half so many times as above or should I be shy?
Lu.

FROM HENRY, COLSTERDALE CAMP 16 AUGUST 1915

Just a line or two to let you know that I arrived back to "our little wet home in the trench" about three o'clock.[63] I arrived at Masham at one o'clock & then had my six miles to tramp in the pouring rain. However, we did it & can do it again. I ran across Harry Taylor at Ripon & a few more Huddersfield fellows whom I knew, who had been over on pass. He was surprised to see me. It has been raining here all day & the camp is in a terrible state. I do not know that I have anything more to tell you at present, but keep a stout heart my sweetheart & don't worry. It has been very very hard to leave you again, but we have had a lovely time whilst I have been over at home, so we must both try & be content for a while. So goodnight my beloved & God bless you. Don't forget to write back, though I know you won't forget.

TELEGRAM: FROM HENRY, COLSTERDALE CAMP 18 AUGUST 1915

Have gone Leeds Recruiting don't send parcel expect me any day Henry

FROM HENRY, LEEDS 19 AUGUST 1915

Just a few lines to let you know that I arrived back alright about a quarter to nine. We have been parading with the Bugle Band this morning, around the streets of Leeds & in front of the Town Hall. We are working from 10 to 12 o'clock, 3.30 to 5, & 7 to 10 at night so we are not doing so bad. We have had our photos taken in City Square, so look in the "Leeds Mercury" to-morrow morning & you might find your humble. I do not know that I have anything more at present, but I will try my best for Sunday.

My address is:-

Pte H Coulter (1570)

c/o Mrs Chadwick,

34 Danby Walk,

Richmond Hill,

Leeds.

FROM LUCY, 20 AUGUST 1915

Thank you very much for your letter, also for the lovely Gladys Cooper postcards, each one you send is nicer than the last, and although you pretend not to admire her, you always choose some lovely cards. I am glad you arrived safe & in good time. When I got back to the shop Marion had just got there, and I did wish I had stayed with you longer, still it can't be helped can it dear, and I am going to look forward to Sunday & hope for the best. Still even if you don't happen to come I must not complain, because I know you always come when you can, and after the lovely surprise of Wednesday I don't think I shall ever grumble again. Oh and it is a consolation to know that for a time at least you are so near to me, it is so much nicer to think of you living in at any rate temporary comfort, than to think of you far away in wretched old Colsterdale, still I wont think about that until you are forced to go back, and I hope for another happy time with you before then. I went up home last night & stayed till half past ten Ma & I do talk when we start, but as it happened Father & Mother had gone to the pictures so nothing was said. I have been thinking about you a great deal to-day & wondering how you were getting on with your recruiting, I smile when I think about it though I cant help it, and I guess you are highly amused at it all, though I did not think you would have to work until ten o'clock it seems rather late does it not. Well I don't think I have much more news so I will close, with fondest love and kisses from

Yours Ever, Lu

P S I expect when you see the kisses you will smile & think I feel brave as I write, but when you come home its altogether different isn't it dear?

FROM HENRY, 34 DANBY WALK, LEEDS 24 AUGUST 1915

Just a few lines to say that I arrived back alright yesterday morning, but you must forgive me sweetheart for not writing you last night, but I was too busy. We were out recruiting in the morning, at the 'Easy Rd Picture Hall' in the afternoon, & at the second house of the Hippodrome at night, so you see we had a rather busy day. We have been out again this morning & are on parade at City Sq. again at 2-45 this afternoon. There is a photograph of us in this morning's 'Mercury' but it is a very poor one. I do not know how long we are staying in Leeds, but think we are going back on Thursday morning. However, they are trying for an extension until Monday, but don't build up on it my darling. It might come off 'crabs.' If we do stay, I shall come home again on Sat night, but I think it is too much to expect. We shall have to 'weight & sea,' my sweetheart, shan't we? …

FROM HENRY, 34 DANBY WALK, LEEDS, 27 AUGUST 1915

Very many thanks for your lovely letter which I received yesterday morning. I am sorry that I did not reply to it last night, but we went to the Empire (instead of Wednesday night) & so I did not get home until late. We were on the stage whilst some officer or other made a speech, so we were highly flattened (sorry, flattered) I can tell you. Afterwards my old friend J H Scotland[64] came & shook hands with us all & wished us 'Good Luck.' And now my darling I have another piece of *'cheerful'* news. We are staying in Leeds until next Wednesday, so I shall be able to come home on Saturday night again, just to plague your dear little life out. I shall be coming by the 9-25 train, due in Hudd'd about 10-30, so you might come & meet me if you will sweetheart. We are only working now from 12 o'clock noon until 1-30 & then again at night from 6-30 until nine o'clock, so it's just like a holiday. We have every afternoon off except Tuesdays & Saturdays, which are Market Days. I do not know that I have much more to write about this time, but I will tell you all my doings of the week, when I see you again to-morrow night.

FROM HENRY, COLSTERDALE CAMP 7 SEPTEMBER 1915

Just a line or two to let you know that I received your ever welcome loving letter this morning; also the cigarettes, & thank you for them very much. I have been in-occulated this morning, & it has been awfull darling. I was done about 10-30 this morning but it has taken hold of me very much & I have been laid just like a log all afternoon until tea-time. However we'll get over it my sweetheart won't we? I am coming home again on Friday until Monday on my in-occulation leave, so we shall have another good time to-gether my darling. You must forgive me not answering your letter in detail my sweetheart but I feel more fit for bed than dabbling in ink. However I will tell you all the news when I come home.

PS I will thank Father personally for the Cigs: when I see him.

FROM HENRY, COLSTERDALE CAMP 12 SEPTEMBER 1915

Just a few lines, as promised, to say that I arrived back alright at the above 'hole,' about 10-30 last night. We just caught the connection at Leeds by about two minutes, so I was not able to come back to Hudd'd as hoped. I know you wanted me to miss the connection you darling & come back until to-morrow morning, but our luck was out sweetheart. It didn't come off did it? Well beauty, I don't know that I have much fresh news to tell you, except that we are going to be in-occulated again next Friday, so should get home on pass again on the following Monday, all being well. I have been to Chapel service this morning, & am writing this about a quarter to two, so I can just picture you going up to Sunday School. We had an hour to wait at Ripon last night, so I went out of the Station & had a look round the town, until our train came. It is a very pretty place & I wish we were stationed there, instead of this 'benighted place.' I am enclosing you two postcards of it, just to give you a slight idea of the place...

FROM HENRY, COLSTERDALE CAMP 14 SEPTEMBER 1915

Very many thanks for your loving letter which I received this morning. I am so sorry to hear of your little disagreeable affair at home, but hope it has blown over by now & that all is serene again. In any case it couldn't have been you, for you are too sweet & lovable to quarrel with anyone, you darling. I think it was just another case of misunderstanding you, as everybody does not understand you beauty as I do. I am going on all right at present. I am waiting patiently for the week-end so that I can be with you again. I am sorry you are feeling so miserable, but you must try & cheer up again for my sake darling. I have just been to a musketry class for N.C.O.'s to-night & think I have framed very fair. (But the last bit should be rubbed out as it's against my principle, except from darling.) I went to the picture-show here last night & it was very fair, besides being quite a change. I forgot to tell you darling on Saturday, but Willie came down on Sat. afternoon just as I was ready to leave & took another snap-shot of me as the other was a failure. He said Gladys was over again for the week-end, so I suppose he would be with her on Sunday. I have not heard from Ma since she went to Manchester, yet, but expect to do so in the morning. Very many thanks darling for your re-assurances of your love for me. They are very dear to me, beloved, & please accept mine in return. I do not know that I have anything fresh to tell you darling, but keep a stout heart & think of me; as I know you do…

FROM LUCY, UNDATED

Thank you very much for your loving sympathising letter which I received this morning, it was just like you to write as you did dear & I thank you very much for all your love & thought for me, and now dear I want to ask you to forgive me for writing such a miserable letter, I am quite ashamed of it now, because it was gloomy, only I was so downhearted & upset I felt as if I must tell you all about it, so burn the old letter dear & forgive me. I am glad you are keeping well dear and I too am waiting & longing for the weekend, but oh dear when I think about Friday & what your visit will cost you I feel ever so sorry for you my brave boy. I know you would do well at the musketry class Henry dear & the last bit need *not* be rubbed out, you will have to get used to praise dear sometime so why not begin now. I am sending a small parcel it seems ages since I sent one, I meant to enclose some Dubbin[65] but left it at the shop, are you short yet? I am sorry the photos were a failure, but am very glad that Willie was just in time to take you again, Mrs Hickman was asking me on Sunday if you had been taken yet. The 3rd & 2nd fifth[66] have left Retford this morning to commence a months route march, the 3/5 left here last night to go to Retford & they are not coming back untill the 17th of October so what a pic-nic they will have, I think the Halifax Territorials[67] are to go as well, so they must be recruiting, anyway they are going to a lot of different towns, so we shant have any soldiers about for a bit. We had a letter from Edgar this morning and he is stationed at North Summercotes the same place as Herbert Shaw so he must be a Medical Board man. I know he had a lot of trouble with his eyes when he was going with Miss Nowell, oh & he is sick of the Army, he says he would like to go to France that seems the general spirit though. You talk Henry dear about my assurances of love, but I can never tell you all that is in my heart and how much I love you I could not do it in a life-time all my thoughts are of you, but you see dear you came into my life and changed it completely, you taught me how to love & accept love in short made me who was a careless, thoughtless, girl the happiest on earth. The trouble at home has not blown over I am sorry to say Mother is friendly but father refuses to have anything to do with his wayward daughter, but I have your love and so I dont mind. I am rather sorry I did not see Gladys this last weekend I should have liked to very much she is such a nice girl, but perhaps I shall do before long. I am going to Gledholt to-morrow night as usual we have four parcels to send this week, because we

collected 16/= on Sunday.[68] I am sorry I shall not be able to
see Ma as usual, I do miss her, but hope she is having a good
time. Well dear I dont think I have any more news so will close
with fondest love & kisses

Yours Lovingly & for Ever Lu.

FROM MRS C TOWNEND, MARLIN[?] HOUSE, SOUTHPORT, UNDATED

Just a few lines to you at last I do hope you will not think it
unkind of me not writing before I have had a hard time with
Mr Townend & arm being broken [ ] I haven't written to you I
have often thought of you in fact you and my two nephews are
never out of my mind and I allways enquire of Lucy every letter
that comes and I do hope that it wont be long before it is all
over and you come home[?] back to us all. Lucy his keeping up
verry well she gets down hearted a bit some times and she will
look at your photo and say Oh Henry if you dont come back
soon I shall go crazy but I try to cheer her up all I can. Dear
Henry you will see by the card that I am staying at Southport for
eight days rest with Mr & Mrs Bevington and the two children
Lucy would have me come for a rest as I was verry much run
down and the rest would do me good so I have left Lucy to
keep house till I return. I got a verry nice letter from her the
other day telling me she would make a splendid house keeper
and I wasnt to worry that is verry good of her. I promised to
write you whilst I was here she will be delighted when I tell
her I have written I hope you will be able to understand I have
got a verry bad Pencil and scarsely any light (what it is to be
in lodgings). No place like home though we are having lovley
weather and it is a verry nice place I must bring my letter to a
close has every one as retired to rest so I must whish you good
night and I hope that God will keep you safe and that you will
soon be with us all before long with fondest love

I remain your affect Mother Mrs C Townend.

To Mrs Townend.

Just a few lines to say that I received Lucy's letter this morning but am terribly upset at the news. I did not think it was as bad as Scarlet Fever, but hope she is improving a bit & trust & pray she will make a speedy recovery.[69] Oh! Mrs Townend, if anything should happen to Lucy I think it would kill me, as she is more to me than life itself. However we shall have to pray to God for her speedy recovery, & hope for the best. I am not coming home to-morrow as expected as I have not yet been in-occulated, but expect being done before long. In the meantime please let me know how Lucy is progressing & give my letters to her; for I do not expect they will let her write (if she was able to) if they have taken her away. Please excuse this letter being scribbled & badly written but I have not got quite over the shock yet.

FROM HENRY, COLSTERDALE CAMP, 25 SEPTEMBER 1915

To Mrs Townend.

Very many thanks for your kind letter which I received on Thursday morning, but you must forgive me for not replying earlier as I have been very busy during the last few days. I am glad that Ma came down to see you & I'm sure she would try & help you all she could during Lucy's illness. I am glad to know that Lucy went cheerfully, but it must have been a hard pull for her to leave home for that wretched old place, but as Ma says in her last letter, perhaps it is all for the best; though I'll be hanged if I can see where the best comes in, at present. However I wrote to her, at the Sanatorium, last night & am going to try & write her a few lines every night, for although she cannot write back in return, I can still keep in touch with her.[70] I should be very, very glad if you will write back to me to-morrow, & let me know how she is progressing, & also if she is in a position to have any Magazines or Papers or Chocolates sent to her yet. I am keeping about all right myself, but am still very much worried with regard to Lucy. However we shall have to have patience & hope for the best. I am enclosing you one or two cards for the Boys, & please give them my kind regards, also Father.

With love for yourself, I remain, Yours affectionately, Henry.

FROM HENRY, COLSTERDALE CAMP 4 OCTOBER 1915

To Mrs C Townend.

Very many thanks for your kind long letter which I received by this morning's post. I was very glad indeed (& much surprised) to learn that you had seen *our 'Lu'* on Saturday & that you were able to talk to her. Also, I am delighted to know that she is improving to the extent of getting up, & trust that she will not be long before she is at home again. You must excuse me not writing before now, but I have had a very busy week-end. We went down to Leeds on Saturday morning for the great recruiting rally in the afternoon, & finished about six in the evening. We had our full pack, including Rifle, (96 lbs in all) to carry around Leeds & Districts. I should think we went about 14 miles in all; that is of course including the six miles from Colsterdale down to Masham Station. We set off, to come back to the 'Wilderness' here, at 7 o'clock last night, out of Leeds & landed up here about half past eleven, absolutely tired out. However, I have had a day's rest to-day to make up for it. I sent Lucy a small parcel of Novels, Papers & Chocolates, from Leeds on Saturday, so I think she should get it alright. I should have come over to Hudd. on Saturday night, but I was quite done up. However, I saw you last Tuesday & there was nothing pressing or else I should have managed to come somehow. I am glad you will let Ma know, when you are going to see Lucy

again, because she will be very, very glad to go with you. I am
enclosing you a few more Cigarette Cards for the Boys. Give
them my love also kind regards to Father…

PS Please write back, when you can spare the time, & let me
know how Lucy is progressing. H.

To Mrs C Townend.

Just a few lines to say that we are still out here in the 'wilds,'
& have not moved yet, as expected. However, we are under
orders to move at any moment; so we shall be going any time
now. Also that I have instructions to proceed to Tynemouth,
nr. Newcastle, on Monday for a course of Field Telegraphy, but
do not know how long I shall be there. However, I will write
you from there & let you know how I am getting on. In the
meantime, I shall be glad to hear from you & also to know how
Lucy is progressing, & whether she will be home for this week-
end or not. I do not know that there is anything else at present,
except that my cold is all about better by now. Hoping you are
all keeping in the best of health & spirits,

I remain, With love, Yours sincerely, Henry.

PS Give my kind regards to Father & the Boys. H.

To Mrs C Townend.

Just a line or two to-day, to say that I am sending a letter (by the
same post as this) to 'Lu,' but am sending it home in the hope
that she has been discharged from the Sanatorium to-day. If not,
then will you please forward it on to her, so that she can get it on
Monday morning. The course of 'Field Telegraphy' at Tynemouth,
(that I told you about in yesterday's letter) is for six weeks, I think,
so I shall not be at home just yet for a little while…

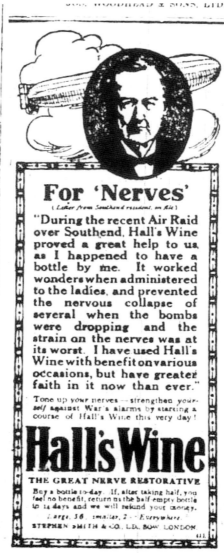

Advertisement for tonic against nervous problems caused by Zeppelins. Lucy and Henry both mention the raids in their letters. (Huddersfield Examiner 1915)

FROM HENRY, ST OSWIN'S HALL, TYNEMOUTH, 15 OCTOBER 1915

My Darling Little Girl,

I was very very glad to receive your welcome and loving letter this (Friday) morning. In fact my heart jumped, when I saw your writing on the envelope. I am so glad you are home again beloved, & I shall feel a lot more easier in my mind, & not as worried about you, as I have been of late. Well darling, I have such a lot to tell you that I scarcely know how to begin. In the first place you must not thank me, for the little I have been able to do, during your very severe illness. What little I have done, is because I love you so dearly, & it has been more than a pleasure to me, to think that I have been able to help just a little. So you must not talk about a great debt being hard to repay, my darling, because there is no debt at all in the first place… Well darling, I'll talk about myself for a bit, because I know you will be anxious to know how I am getting on. I am keeping quite well of myself, & I keep plodding away nicely. I am up here for about five weeks, & in that time, have to learn, wire jointing, the 'Morse Code' (& pass out at the 'Exam' at 8 words a minuet), 'Semaphore' (that is signalling with flags, & have to pass out at 12 words a minuet) & Map Reading. So I think I have my hands full darling (In addition to this I have to eat, sleep & breathe; so it doesn't leave me much time to do much else, doesn't it?) I passed my wire jointing 'Exam' this morning (both on the Single and Cable Wire) with a possible 10 marks out of 10; so I've made a good start anyhow, choose what kind of a mess I make at the other Exams later on. However we shall have to trust to luck & 'weight & sea.' I dare say you will have read in the Papers about the big Zeppellin raid on London, on Wednesday night.[71] Well, when we got in, on that night, we were told to sleep ready dressed, in case of emergency; as they had received news at the Wireless Station, that 8 Zepps had been seen coming over to England (making southwards) & we had to get ready for a raid. So all the guns were uncovered on Spanish Battery (that is just between our huts & the sea) & the gunners got busy. There are 2-six in. 2-nine inch & 2 twelve inch guns on the Battery; besides a dozen others that are hidden away in the cliffs somewhere. Well we went to bed in the dark (as they had turned all the electricity off) but we were soon awakened by our guns firing at something out at sea; but we could see nothing. When it was daylight, we saw a Warship & two Submarines lying in the harbour. It appears they had been chasing two Zepps during the night, but they had got away in the darkness. There are 7 men to each gun, so you can tell there are a good few soldiers stationed up here. The place is full of them & officers. They are dredging the river, at the mouth, to enable them to launch another 'Dreadnought' ('not ours' at home[72]) further up the river at Newcastle; sometime next week. I do not know whether it will get into the papers; but it is common news up here. There are about 150 of us here to learn Signalling, & they come (as representatives) from nearly every regiment in England. There are the Scottish Bantams, Notts & Derbys, Tyneside Scottish, The Leicesters, East Yorks, West Yorks, & one from the 2nd/5th (Hudd Territorials) & Hudd R.F.A. There are also a good few of the 1st/5th (Hudd) Territorials here; who have been in action, got wounded, & sent up here to recuperate; so you see, darling, I am not by myself. I am the only representative of the 17th W.Y. so I feel highly flatten'd (sorry flattered.) There are two Submarines & two Destroyers stationed at the mouth of the river, & they stop every boat as it enters the harbour. It's quite laughable sometimes to watch them; because they all blow their whistles, sirens, gongs & bells & anything else they happen to have; & try to make the biggest noise in creation. And they manage to succeed, sometimes, for the noise is deafening. There were 6 Danish Ships & two French Destroyers came in this morning,

& they passed so close that we could see all the people on the deck; from the top of the cliffs. I am glad you have not to go to work just yet, darling, but I think you will be stronger after your illness. At least that's what Ma thinks. However, you must take great care of yourself; for my sake, & be strong & well again, for when I come home again…

FROM HENRY, ST OSWIN'S HALL, TYNEMOUTH, 16 OCTOBER 1915

Enclosed please find a small present as a token of my love & devotion for you. I am also sending you a P.C. or two of Tynemouth, just to give you a slight idea of what the place is like. The one of 'The Cliffs' is where we are stationed at present, & shows our huts in the background. I am also sending you a Novel or two, as I know you will want something to do, to while away the time, during the next fortnight. Also a P.C. of *our?* old 'heroine' – G.C.[73] (Sorry I can't find one of George Formby; or I would have sent that too) There are all Lady Conductors on the buses here, & I have seen a few Lady Drivers this morning. However, I have not been on the cars yet, as I'm not fully insured. We finished to-day (Sat) at 12 o'clock noon, until 9-30 Monday morning; but I wish you were here with me darling. What a time we should have, shouldn't we? However, we shall have to wait until I get nearer Huddersfield; as I'm nearly up in Scotland at present…

FROM HENRY, ST OSWIN'S HALL, TYNEMOUTH, 19 OCTOBER 1915

I was very, very glad to receive your welcome loving letter this morning & to know you are getting strong & well again… And now, sweetheart, I will tell you a little of how I am getting on. On Saturday night I went down to the Comedy Variety Theatre at North Shields & it was a sell. Talk about a third rate house; it was a thirty-third & the artists were 133rd. Charlie

Chaplin or Fred Karno's Co.[74] wasn't in it compared to this.
It was awful. We have seen *some* turns at the Palace, but they
were pic-nics compared to these. The first turn on was a Lady
Singer; but she would have been far better in a home. I think
it would have been a far far better thing, if she had never
come on. She sang like a 'Chip on a plate' or else a flag at
half mast. The next was a commedian. He should have been
inoculated with the first turn. He deserved it. The next turn
was the Gaumont Graphic, & the next was three tramps who
represented Rag-time. That did it. I could stand it no longer,
so I came out properly fed up. On Sunday morning I went
to Chapel; & in the afternoon went to North Shields again
& crossed the river (by Ferry) over to South Shields. Nearly
about the size of Leeds I should imagine. There are plenty of
Music Halls & Picture Palaces & my old friend the one & only
'G. F.'[75] is at the top of the 'Empire' bill, so I shall have to go
down again on Saturday night, as I did not get to Newcastle to
see him. You would laugh at the dialect up here at Tynemouth.
They talk so fast that you can't make out what on earth they
are talking about. They start low & finish up at the end, about
three octaves higher. Also, when they ask you a question they
answer it for you with the same breath. If they ask you if you
like Tynemouth, they say:- 'Do you like Tynemouth No?' And
of course you give them the inevitable reply 'Yes, I think so, no
I'm sure.' On Sunday night I had a walk along the Promenade
to Whitley Bay, about three miles away, & came back by Car.[76]
(But it wasn't a Lady Driver. No jolly fear.) We have some good
fun in our hut between the Durham Light Infantry & the West
Yorks. We call them Scotch Thistles, & they call us 'Yorkshire
Pudden-Heads;' whatever the latter might mean. Still it's all in
the game & we've only broken three windows so far. Of course
we've hopes for more. I am glad that you went up home on

Sunday, darling, & kept Ma company. It would cheer her up I know, & I want you to go up as often as you will sweetheart…

Just a few lines in reply to your letter which I received alright yesterday dinner-time. I should have replied to it last night, but the Y.M.C.A. was full when I went in, so I could not get to reply to it. I hope you enjoyed the Palladium on Wednesday night & also that you remembered me to Luke & Leah when you went up to Elland yesterday. I am not at all surprised to hear about Marion & H.W. parting company. The wonder is, how they have managed to keep in so long… I have found two more 'G.C.'s' to-day & am enclosing them along with this letter. I do not know whether the set of her that you had, had to be destroyed when they were disinfecting your house[77], but if they were, please let me know, & I will try & get another collection together. And now darling, there has a very 'disastrous' thing occurred. I sent a parcel home to Ma last Monday morning, containing a few of my things that I had no further use for at present, & a large bundle of letters with two or three rubber bands around them. They were all the letters that I had received since I enlisted & there would be about 200 in number. They were mostly from you & Ma. Well Ma writes to say that she received the parcel, but it was burst open when she got it, & the letters were missing. What's to be done? All my lovely love-letters gone astray & if anyone should read them they will smile won't they sweetheart. However, I have been to the G.P.O. here at Tynemouth & have filled a form in to-day, so we shall have to wait & see results. It is both laughable & lamentable & I don't know whether to smile or roar. Which shall I do darling? I went on the stone pier yesterday & up to the Lighthouse which is at the end; & came back by a passage under the Sea, which they use in stormy weather to get to the

Lighthouse from the shore. It is all fitted up with Electric Light & is very interesting. I finish my course up here on the 8th of November (which is a fortnight on Monday) but I am going to write for a pass home for two or three days, before I join my regiment again. I do not know whether I shall get it or not, but I think I am entitled to a pass, as I have not had one since the beginning of September...

FROM HENRY, ST OSWIN'S HALL, TYNEMOUTH, 24 OCTOBER 1915

Very many thanks for your loving letter which I received quite safely this morning. I am still getting on alright, but it has turned very cold up here & the sea is very rough. It seems to throw the vessels about just like cockle-shells & as we watch them it seems marvellous how they manage to keep up... I am very very sorry about the letters being lost, but really it is humourous sweetheart, & the more I think about it, the more I smile to myself. I am also glad that you see it in the same light as I do, because I thought you might be vexed with me. It is really my fault for not wrapping them up more secure; but how on earth was I to know that they were going astray, darling. However, I have had a circular this morning from the Post Office People, saying they were looking into the matter, as I hope they will turn up for I value yours so much. I am glad you liked the Gladys Coopers', but I might be able to come across another one or two more that you haven't got, before I leave Tynemouth. I went down to South Shields last night, intending to see Gladys Cooper's rival in 'Beauty' at the Empire there; but could not get in although it was 6 o'clock when I got there. So I went to the Theatre Royal instead & saw a play entitled 'The Woman Who Did Tell' & it was quite pathetic, I assure you. I think if you had been there you would have wept, but I would not have minded that, if I could of only had you with me. I went to Chapel this morning; for a walk on the Promenade this afternoon, & am stopping in to-night to write this to you, so you see how I fill my Sundays in. It is about eight o'clock as I am finishing this letter to you, & I can just immagine you coming out of Chapel, darling...

FROM HENRY, ST OSWIN'S HALL, TYNEMOUTH, 28 OCTOBER 1915

...I passed my second Exam last Monday with another 10 marks out of the possible 10, so I'm still going strong. (Choose how long it lasts; as I have another six Exams to come off next week.) I know you will be pleased as I am darling; & I think that it's your love (& pretty face) that pulls me through. Still, I think you will know best, so I leave it to you sweetheart. It has been a wretched day here, to-day, & it has done nothing else but rain, rain, rain & the sea is so rough that it throws it half way up the Cliffs; when the tide comes up. There has been a very big fire here to-day, & the worst of it was, it happened at one of the houses on the Prom. that has been turned into a Military Hospital for the Wounded Soldiers. However they got them all out in time, though the place was gutted. It was very exciting & it seems a wonder, it was not worse than it was. I am glad you went up to have tea with Ma last Sunday darling, & I can just picture you there (as I write this) with our 'Dreadnought' purring away on the rug. I wish I had been there, sweetheart, to complete the picture, but we shall have to wait until I can get home again. Also I do *not* think you are going on the downward path through missing Sunday School. You are a little angel darling & I can never thank you enough for looking after Ma, the same as you have done... I note what you say about John Armitage joining the 'Green Howards'[78] & can only say good luck to him. The representative from that Regiment, who is up here learning Signalling, happens to be a Huddersfield fellow, so I have mentioned it to him about John joining, & he says he will look him up as soon as he gets back

to Otley. So I think he will get along all right… I am not at all
surprised to hear that the Hudd. R.F.A. are due to go out, & I
almost wish I was going with them. They will catch it rather
lively, I think, especially if they are sent to relieve Serbia.[79] Still,
good luck to them, & may they all come safely home again;
which is very improbable. There seems to have been quite an
epidemic of Babies around the Birkby District lately, according
to your letter. I don't wish Mrs Roberts' any harm, but I hope
hers keeps them all up every night in the week, & that it's as
cross as it can be when it cuts its teeth. She's such a cheerful
soul & she [has] been so friendly with us all lately, hasn't she
darling? Still, may her troubles be little ones, & all her little
ones a trouble…

FROM HENRY, ST OSWIN'S HALL, TYNEMOUTH, 2 NOVEMBER 1915

Just a few lines to try and thank you for your lovely Birthday
Present, which I received quite safely this morning; & also your
Card & Best Wishes for my Birthday. Oh Sweetheart it was
a beautiful present & I can't thank you enough for it; but I
am sure you will understand. It is one more little action to
strengthen the bond between us, & which no one will ever
break. I found the little note inside the Box, & thank you for
the love & regard you have for me. You don't know how I feel
to-night as I write this to you darling; but I feel somehow so
thankful that I have your love & that you are all to me. I really
cannot thank you on paper as I should; but I will thank you
personally as soon as I can get home. I also received the P.C.
from Father & Mother & also the one (& Cigarettes) from
Henry; so please thank them dear on my behalf. I have worn
the Watch all day & it goes splendidly & all the fellows have
admired it. It will be very useful too & also a constant reminder
of you my beloved, as if I could ever forget you for an hour, & I
shall treasure it always. I think I have had a very happy Birthday

sweetheart, considering that I am so far away from home. I had
7 Post-Cards & 2 Parcels & the Postman wanted to know if I
had a Mail-Bag of my own… I think I am going on alright,
but it is rather hard work as we are having two Examinations
a day, & it is a bit of a strain. We have had six up to to-night
& I have 58 out of a possible 60 marks, so I think I might
possibly pull through yet. You see the limit of each Exam is 10
points, so I have 4 tens & 2 nines. However, we have six more
to go yet, so we shall have to wait and see how I come out at
the end. I am trying for my Certificate, but shall have to trust
to my lucky? star & think of you. We had rather an exciting
incident this dinner-time that I must tell you about before I
close. As I have told you before, sweetheart, every boat that
comes in the Harbour is stopped by the examination boats,
before it is allowed to come up the River. Well, this dinner-
time one refused to stop & hence the trouble began. We were
all having our dinner about 1 o'clock, when bang, one of the
9 in Guns in the Battery went off. It shook the Hut & rattled
all the pots & of course brought us all outside to see what
the trouble was. It seems that they had signalled it to stop &
when it had refused, sent a shot across its bows as a kind of a
gentle warning. But the thing didn't end here, for the blessed
thing fired back but didn't fire far enough as the shell fell into
the Sea. Of course there was nothing else to do but fire again
from the Battery & this they did in no time. And then one of
the 6 in guns spoke from by the Wireless Station & also a new
Gun-Boat (that has only been launched from Newcastle this
morning & was having a trial trip down to the Sea) had a turn.
But the noise was deafening darling although they only fired
one shot apiece. And then the noise must have attracted all the
boats as three Submarines came racing down the river from
Newcastle, with two Torpedo Boats following. The last we saw
of it, was with all these boats around it with about half a dozen

Clipstone Camp near Mansfield. A sea of wooden huts housed thousands of troops under training, including Henry. (Pauline Marples)

examination boats thrown in, so I don't know how it went on as it was time for us to parade again. We really thought the German Fleet had broken out of the Keil Canal this time, & was paying us a visit. But I noticed that the three Submarines & two Torpedo Boats were still there when we came in to tea, so perhaps there is something doing to-night. Let's hope so. And now, my darling, I really must come to a close, or I shall never catch the post to-night & I want you to get this in the morning.

FROM LUCY, 3 NOVEMBER 1915

Thank you very much for your ever welcome loving letter which I received this morning. It was a lovely letter dear & I thank you very much for it, but you must not thank me so much, you know dear you would not let me thank you for the Chocalates you sent, and besides it was the least I could do when I love you so much. I am very glad that you like it though that was what troubled me most. When I went to see Ma last Thursday night, she asked me what I thought would be a suitable present for you & between us we decided on a Fountain Pen, and so she asked me to meet her in town on Friday afternoon, so I did & we bought it then, of course she asked me to go back with her to tea & of course I did. After tea we had ever such fun putting the almond paste on your cake & getting it to stick, so you see how busy we were, then we went up Marsh shopping & I saw Teddy serving a customer but he did not see me. Of course I did not say anything in the letter I scribbled on Saturday night because we thought it would spoil the fun. I am glad you had a card from the little ones at Manchester, the dear little things think the world of you. I am sorry you are having to work so hard just now dear and I quite understand that so many Exams must be a terrible strain, but I think you have done splendidly & I am so proud of you & I know you will pull through all right. With regard to those songs that you asked about, they were not destroyed dear, I have them all just as you wrote them, & fancy you saying they could have suffered a worse fate, oh! you are a terror and really they are all very good & I wont have you talking about them like that. I commenced work on Monday morning & up to now have enjoyed myself ever so much. I feel better than I have done for ages & everyone thinks I look ever so well. I do hope you will be able to come home before going back to Colsterdale, there has been quite a lot of soldiers in town this week-end & they make me feel so lonely I want you so much, but there I'm not going to be a baby. Have you heard anything more of the missing letters, I have not seen Ma since Sunday so I don't know whether the inspector has been again or not. I am glad you have heard something about the Photos I had given them up as lost. What excitement there has been since you went to Tynemouth, what with air raids and one thing or another. I think the boat must have belonged to the enemy or it would have stopped when challenged, and I am very much afraid that the firing would have made me terribly nervous. Mr Waterworth told me this dinner time that the 17th West Yorks were going to Leeds next week I don't know wether there is any truth in it or not. But really I must stop. I expect you will be quite sleepy by now, so Goodnight & sweet dreams my sweetheart,

with fondest love & kisses I remain Yours for Eternity, Lu.

FROM HENRY, ST OSWIN'S HALL, TYNEMOUTH, 5 NOVEMBER 1915

Just a few lines in reply to your welcome loving letter which I received yesterday morning. The course here finishes to-morrow (Sat.) & I think I have got through alright but it has been a big strain. We had 5 Examinations on Wednesday & 2 long ones yesterday, to bring them to a close. We have had a day's holiday to-day & I think we have earned it. I wrote to my Captain, last Tuesday night, asking him to send my return Railway Warrant & also for two or three days leave at home; but up to the present I have received no reply. However, it might come in the morning, but if it doesn't I shall be in a fix, as I shall be all about stranded here. If it should come, I shall try to get home until Monday at the least, you may depend upon that, & in that case I will come to meet you at 8-30. That is, of course, if I get my Warrant or not in the morning. I had one of the officials from the G.P.O. at Tynemouth here yesterday & he brought me the missing letters. I signed for them & asked him where they had been, but he could not tell me. However, it's a relief to get them back & I have put them at the bottom of my Kit-Bag, as I'm not going to trust them to the tender mercies of the Post Office people again, in a hurry…

PS The Watch is going splendidly & keeps good time, so I am finding it very useful already. H.

One of the YMCA huts at Clipstone Camp. Note the writing paper spread out on the tables. Henry spent many hours in these huts writing to Lucy on YMCA notepaper. (Pauline Marples)

Henry apparently managed a short leave in Huddersfield, before rejoining his training battalion at a different camp. Clipstone Camp was built on the outskirts of Mansfield, Nottinghamshire, on ground owned by the Duke of Portland. The first troops had arrived in May 1915, and by June the next year there was accommodation for about 60,000 troops.[80] Note that Henry has been promoted to Lance Corporal, the lowest non-commissioned rank.

FROM HENRY, D COMPANY, 19TH BN, WEST YORKSHIRE REGIMENT, CLIPSTONE CAMP, NEAR MANSFIELD, 11 NOVEMBER 1915

Just a line or two to let you know that I arrived here alright about 5-30. I had to change at Penistone & then went on to Worksop (through Sheffield) & then had to change on to the Midland for Mansfield. The camp is about 4 miles from Mansfield but they run a service of motor cars between there & the Camp, so you haven't it to walk as at Colsterdale. I have found Willie & he is going on alright. They sent him up to

Colsterdale & then back here to Clipstone as I thought they would. It seems to be a very big Camp, but I haven't seen much of it yet. The post leaves here at 6 o'clock, so you won't get this until to-morrow night. I think this is all this time but I will write again to-morrow all being well.

My address is:-

(1570) L/C H Coulter,

'D' Co., 19th West Yorks,

Clipstone Camp,

Nr. Mansfield.

(Notts.)

PS Please excuse scribble. H.

FROM HENRY, CLIPSTONE CAMP, 12 NOVEMBER 1915

Just a few lines as promised in my letter to you of last night. We have been removing again to-day to about 2 miles nearer Mansfield, & it has been a job & no mistake. It started to rain here last night about 8 o'clock & it has never ceased since, & the Camp is in a terrible state being about 6 inches of mud & water. It is 2 miles long & 8 miles round, so you can immagine what a size it is. There are about 50,000 Troops here of all Regiments, 6 Y.M.C.A.'s & also a Salvation Army Hut.[81] I do not know that I have much more news to tell you except that Willie is in the same hut as me & I think he seems a little bit sickened of it all but he will soon get over that. You must excuse my last letter & this being rather short, darling, but I will write you longer ones when I am more settled. Give my love to Mother & kind regards to Father & the Boys.

FROM HENRY, CLIPSTONE CAMP, 14 NOVEMBER 1915

Just a few lines to let you know that I am still getting along alright, & liking this place a lot better than at Colsterdale. I

FROM HENRY, CLIPSTONE CAMP, 24 NOVEMBER 1915 (WEDNESDAY)

Very many thanks for your long loving letter which I received by first post this morning. It has been a long time coming; since Monday, but it has arrived at last. Well sweetheart, in the first place I am suffering from a very severe cold. I went to the Doctor yesterday morning & he examined me & then sent me back to bed. I stayed in bed all day & then got up at night to write a letter to Ma in reply to hers that I received yesterday. However I was awake nearly all night coughing, so I went to him again this morning & he said that I'd got influenza & ordered me two days' rest. However, please don't worry darling, as I am getting on all right, & will soon be better. I am glad you liked the Gladys Coopers alright also the Photo of myself & a few more of Fred Karno's & Walter Bird's Co. Ltd. I was sorry to hear about Bertie Thorpe's death, but you know sweetheart he died for his country & that is what we are all prepared to do if need's must. He could not have died better. Also I was sorry to hear about Percy's friend although I never met him. I am glad you went up to spend the day with Ma last Sunday, darling, & that you had a good time. And now, my beloved, you must excuse me this time for not writing you as long a letter as usual, but I must come to a conclusion as I don't feel equal to writing any more to-night, & must get back to bed before the Doctor misses me. So goodnight, my darling, & God bless you. PS Give my love to Mother & all at home; & I will write you again to-morrow if at all possible.

FROM HENRY, CLIPSTONE CAMP, 25 NOVEMBER 1915

Just a few lines to-day, to follow up my letter of last night, as promised. In the first place, sweetheart, I want you to let me thank you (& Mother) for the lovely parcel which I received quite safely, by this morning's post. Also the loving letter &

'Examiner' inside. It is very very good of you both & I can never thank you enough. I was very sorry to hear about Herbert Ainley's death, & I knew him very well. The Marsh boys seem to have been catching it pretty hot lately, don't they darling? But we'll try & avenge them when we get out. At least that is the general opinion here, but it's a long time coming off. But let's talk about something more cheerfull. I am glad you all liked the Novelty Postcard. I'll admit its very funny & you couldn't help but smile when you saw it. It is still very cold here yet, beloved, but my 'Flu' has nearly left me & I'm quite 'calm' at present. I have got up again to-day, darling, as I'm about fed up with being in bed. I hope you liked hearing Edward French last night beauty. How I wish I could have been with you, how happy we both should have been. Of course I remember our Wednesday afternoon walks, my darling. How could I ever forget anything that you were connected in, beloved? That would be quite impossible. But although I miss them & you, so much now, yet our love is stronger then ever, & I shall always bless the day when I first met you. I loved you from the first Lucy, & shall love you to the end & beyond that… I am enclosing you a Camp Magazine which I think will amuse you & also a Card or two for the boys.[86]

FROM HENRY, CLIPSTONE CAMP, 2 DECEMBER 1915

…I had a small parcel containing an 'Examiner' & a pair of Mittens from Ma, by yesterday's post; but I suppose you will be up at home to-night (being Thursday) & Ma will be telling you. I put in for a pass, yesterday, for this week-end, but unfortunately have not received one as I am wanted for Garrison Duty in the Camp, and so could not have one; but I am pretty certain for one, for next week-end. Willie has got one, however, so he will be coming home to-morrow night, as the passes from here, are from Friday until Sunday night.

He says he will call & see Ma about Sunday tea-time, so if you would like to see him (and Gladys) slip in home about that time. I am sorry that I could not manage one, also, but I think we can wait in patience another week, my sweetheart. I am sorry to hear about Frank Holland, but hope he will make a speedy recovery. I note what you say about holding a Memorial Service for Bert Thorpe at Gledholt a week on Sunday, & think I should like to go. However, we shall see. I have nearly a tin of Dubbin left yet, sweetheart, so am not really in need of any yet, but thank you all the same… I have not heard anything about Teddy either, lately. Perhaps he's enlisted. (I wonder.) We went for a Route March into Mansfield, yesterday morning, and in the afternoon, we went Bayonet Fighting. You know what that is darling. That pleasant little pastime of sticking bayonets into sacks hanging down & filled with straw, & pretending they are Germans. Quite a lovely pastime isn't it darling? But I suppose you'll shrug your Shoulders & say 'Ugh!' you beauty…

FROM HENRY, CLIPSTONE CAMP, 5 DECEMBER 1915

Just a few lines in answer to your loving letter which I received last night, by the last post. Well darling, I am still 'existing', that is, going on alright, I think. We had a dreadful day here yesterday, & I got a nice soaking. Rain, Rain & more Rain. I was Orderley Corporal too, into the bargain, so had to be out in it, nearly all day. However, it's all in the game so we can't grumble, can we? I have been on my own since Willie went on pass, but expect him back to-night. (If he lands.) I was very much interested, dear, to hear about your Canadian Cousin coming, & should have liked to have met him. Also his Indian friend, but you dear little goose, do you mean Indian or 'Red' Indian when you talk about feathers & war-paint. I can just fancy Mother having a fit if he should happen to be a Red Indian. What a surprise! But there he will have come by

The Guard House at Clipstone Camp. A 24-hour guard was maintained in the camp from this building. Henry mentions an occasion when he was Corporal of the Guard. (Pauline Marples)

now, so you will know what he is like. I am writing this at the Y.M. at Mansfield, & as I have a late pass, I think I shall have tea here & then go to the Pictures to-night, as they open here on Sundays, at 8 o'clock. I am Corporal of the Guard in the morning, so you will think about me during the long hours of Monday night, my beloved, as I shall be thinking about you. I am enclosing you the latest Souvenir Brooch & also a Card or two, & hope you will like them. I have not seen Alfred Lilley & Co since last Monday, but I dare say I shall be running across them again, before long. I was rather surprised to hear that 'Lawrence,' had enlisted, but you do not say in what Regiment, darling. I hope you will meet Gladys & Willie, up at home to-day & should have liked to have been there also; but cheer up sweetheart, perhaps I shall be next Sunday. And now, my darling, I really must be coming to a close; as it is nearly tea-time; but write back to-morrow night, (if you can spare the time) & tell me all the news. With love to all at Home,

FROM HENRY, CLIPSTONE CAMP, 8 DECEMBER 1915

Just a few lines in reply to your loving letter which I received this tea-time. I think I am getting on alright & keeping in good health. Your letter seems to have been a long time in coming, darling, but it came round by Nottingham, so perhaps that will account for it. I came off guard yesterday morning at 9-30 & was just about fagged out. However I slept until tea-time to make up for it, so feel about alright again in that respect. I am glad that your Cousin came on Sat. alright & hope he is having a good time. I should have liked to have seen him, but as he leaves to-morrow (Thursday) I shall just miss him if I come home on pass on Friday night. (Although that is by no means certain as we are very short of N.C.O.'s) Still I will try my best. I heard from Alfred Lilley that Lawrence Bower has joined the Royal Engineers, & also that Harry has joined as well. I had a letter from Ma on Monday & she said that you had not been up on Sunday, but she was expecting Willie. Willie returned here on Sunday night & says he enjoyed himself very much whilst he was at home. He said that he called & saw Ma on Sunday tea-time & that she was very pleased to see him & Gladys. Also that Gladys was very much disappointed that you was not there. However, it can't be helped. And now, darling, I must come to a close, but if I should get a pass this week-end, I will try & let you know. Give my love to all at home, & also my best wishes to your Cousin, & tell him that I hope to meet him in the trenches, with a bit of luck.

FROM HENRY, CLIPSTONE CAMP, 13 DECEMBER 1915

Just a few lines to say that I arrived back at Camp about 3-30. I had to change at Mirfield, Normanton, Chesterfield & Tye Bridge & then on to Mansfield; so you can guess I was just about fed up by the time I reached the latter place. Well, sweetheart, I have to see the Captain at 7-30 in the morning, but don't you worry, my beloved, I'll get through all right.[87] Anyhow, I will let you know in my next letter how I go on. I have seen Willie & he is getting on alright; but he seems to be more worried about me, than what I am about myself. Still it's done now, dearest, so it can't be helped can it? I think we have both had a lovely time this week-end (as we always have when I come home) so it will have been worth it if I get 'C.B.' for the duration of the war. Still I don't think it will be as bad as that. But not a word to Ma, my beloved. You know she'd only worry, & besides 'where ignorance is bliss, tis folly to be wise.' I hope you will go up to-night after you have finished packing Parcels at Gledholt…

FROM HENRY, CLIPSTONE CAMP, 16 DECEMBER 1915

Just a few lines to say that I received your long loving letter by first post this morning, & thank you very, very much for it. And now, my beloved, I have a little bit of news for you. In the first place, darling, I was 'stabbed' again yesterday. That is to say in plain English, that I was in-oculated yesterday, for the second time, at 2-30 in the afternoon, on the 15th of December in the year of our Lord, 1915. I was going to write & tell you last night, but I felt so very sore that I really couldn't, so you must forgive me, my beloved. I feel a lot better to-day, but am still very stiff & sore. Willie was done as well, & he says he feels about the same. I am very, very, sorry to have to disappoint you, darling, but I can't get home for Christmas, as I should have liked to have done. There are four batches of us to go for 6 days' leave, & they are to begin next Wednesday. However, I am down to go with the second batch, which starts on the 28th, so I shall be home for New Year all being well. Poor Willie does not go until the 10th of Jany. which is when the fourth lot starts. I know you will be terribly disappointed, my beloved, (as I am myself) but do not be vexed with me, darling, as I tried my best to get Christmas. With regard to my overstaying my pass last week-end, I told the Captain that I stayed behind on the Sunday to go to a memorial Service in honour of two of my friends who have been killed at the front. He said – 'Alright, don't let it occur again,' and then let me off with a caution; so I think I came out very lucky, darling. But not a word to Ma, you beauty. I was very much amused at your brother's dream; but you know dearest, as well as I do, that it's only the forecast of what is going to happen when this blessed War is over. That is, of course, if you will have an 'old Soldier.' I shall be glad to receive my Christmas Parcel from the good friends at Gledholt; & shall look forward to it more than ever, now that I cannot get home. But we will have our Christmas at New Year this time, darling. I have not seen Alfred Lilley & Co., since I came of pass last Monday, but I am going down to the Y.M. to-night, so might run across them there, but I won't breathe a word about the Parcels, darling, I promise you. I am glad that John Willie has got the management of your Shop, & tell him from me, that I wish him the best of luck in his new career…

FROM HENRY, CLIPSTONE CAMP, 19 DECEMBER 1915

Just a line or two to let you know that I have got over the effects of my inoculation, & feel about all serene again now. Well, sweetheart, I received the parcel from Gledholt alright, this morning, & thank you, & all the folk at Gledholt, for sending the same to me. It is very good of you all, & shows that I am not quite forgotten at Gledholt yet. Willie & I are down at the Y.M.C.A. here at Mansfield & have just seen Alfred Lilley & Co. They tell me they have also received their parcels, by this morning's post; & seem very pleased with them. I am enclosing you a Photo of Willie, (& two more of Fred Karno's Co.) & also another, which I think you will like. *I* have done the deed to-day; & they will be ready on Tuesday. (That is, if the Photographer survives to print them; after he has once seen the plate. D.V.[88]) (God willing.) However, you shall have one, my darling, choose how bad they are. That is, of course, if you think you can stand it. Well, my beloved, it will soon be Christmas, & we're here; but I suppose we shall have to make the best of a bad job. So cheer up & dry those pretty eyes of yours, you darling. I do not know that there is anything more at present, but I am dying to hear from you, beloved, for it seems such a long time since I did. But you see I love you so much, darling, & that makes all the difference. I had a letter from Ma by this morning's post, in which she tells me that she is thinking of going to Manchester to spend Xmas; but I suppose she will be telling you about it. And now, my darling, I must be coming to a close; but I *do* wish you were here with me to-night, you beauty...

FROM HENRY, CLIPSTONE CAMP, 20 DECEMBER 1915

Your loving letter received this morning, by first post. I am going on alright I think & was so glad to hear from you, sweetheart; but you have been so very busy lately, that of course I forgive you. (I couldn't do anything else, could I?) I wrote you a letter last night from the Y.M.C.A. at Mansfield, but I dare say you will have got that by now. I want you to thank Mr Hall, on my behalf, when you see him darling, for the parcel from Gledholt, & tell him I am enjoying myself & the contents very much. (That is to say by 'enjoying' that I am still 'existing.') I am glad that you went to see Ma last night, for I know she would be glad to see you, my darling. She thinks the world about you. By the way, I saw the writing on the parcel from Gledholt, & recognized it as yours, sweetheart. How good you are to me, my beloved. I can't think how I came to deserve it, but I'm afraid you make far too much of me. I am not the only

Soldier in the Army, darling, you know, & there are far better men at present, than I can ever hope to be. Still, I am very, very lucky to possess your love darling, & you know, very well, that I love you just as much in return. Willie & I went to the pictures again last night (Sunday) & enjoyed them very much. There was only one drawback; & that was your absence darling. Still, I know you would be thinking of me, as I thought of you, & longing for the time when we should both be together again. I note what you say about Harry Taylor being over on leave, & am sorry he looks so worried & ill. Perhaps Soldiering does not agree with him; or else it's the thought of going out to the front. It will seem funny to you, darling, having John Willie for a manager, but I suppose you will get used to it in time. And now, my beloved, I must really be coming to a close as it is getting late, & I want to catch the post to-night so that you will get this in the morning.

FROM HENRY, CLIPSTONE CAMP, 24 DECEMBER 1915

Just a few lines to say that I received your lovely present by last night's post & thank you ever so much for it. It was a lovely gift sweetheart & is just what will come in very handy for me. I think I shall start keeping a diary, darling, on the 1st of next year, & propose that you do the same; & then we exchange them (for each other to read) every time I come home on leave. What do you think of the idea, darling? Let me know in your next letter. I received the little parcel from Marion, quite safely by this morning's post; & I want you to thank her for me. And now, my beloved, I have a little disappointment for you. I am sorry to say that I cannot come home next Tuesday as expected; but have to wait until the following Monday instead; which is the 3rd of Jany. The reason is, that the Railway Company cannot carry as many troops as expected; so we are having to go in 8 batches instead of 4, as before arranged. I do hope you won't mind, my beloved, for it cannot be helped can it? I am a lot better off than Willie, however, who cannot go until the last lot, which goes sometime in Feby. I do not know that I have anything more this time; but please excuse scribble as I am very busy at present. Give my love to all at home, & also my best wishes for a Merry Christmas & a Prosperous New Year.

PS Many thanks, darling, for the Christmas Card you enclosed. It is a very nice one.

FROM HENRY, CLIPSTONE CAMP, 25 DECEMBER 1915

Just a few lines to-night, as I feel as if I must write to you, dearest, as I have been thinking of you all day, & wondering what kind of a Christmas you are spending. Willie as gone down to Mansfield & as I cannot go with him, being Orderley Corporal, I am left all alone. And I do feel lonely to-night, sweetheart, somehow. I suppose it must be because it is Christmas night & you are not with me my beloved. It is 7 o'clock as I write this to you & I have just been thinking of another Christmas Night, 12 months ago. I think we went to see 'Joseph in the land of Egypt,' at the Picturedrome[89] on that night, didn't we darling? What a difference to-night. But there, I think I must be getting downhearted, darling, & I shall be getting you downhearted too & that will never do. I have been very busy today, sweetheart, (& for the last two days also) as one of the duties of the Orderley Corporal is to look after (& deliver) all letters & parcels; so you can guess I have had shoals of letters & sacks of parcels to look after this Christmas. I have also the bread, meat, butter, tea etc to supervise & see that each hut gets its proper quantity of each. Also to see that each Officer gets his Orders (which are Typewritten) for the following day; & also attend with the Doctor whilst he interviews the Sick. So you can guess that I am kept 'some' busy. Then at 9-30 at night I have to attend Staff Parade & report all correct for the

Advertisement for the Picturedrome cinema, Huddersfield, where Henry and Lucy often went.
Note the offer of free seats for War Hospital patients.
(Huddersfield War Hospital Magazine 1917)

day. After which I can go to bed (until 6-30 the following morning) & dream about the sweetest little girl in the whole world, & of the time when I shall have her all to myself & try to make her as happy as she is lovely. So goodnight, my darling, & God bless you & keep you safe for me. Give my love to Mother & all at home.

FROM HENRY, CLIPSTONE CAMP, 27 DECEMBER 1915

Just a few lines to say that I received your loving, welcome letter, yesterday morning, & thank you very much for it. I am sorry that I did not reply to it yesterday, but Willie & I had a trip over to Alfreston (which is about 10 miles from here) & had our tea at Percy's young lady's. Percy was over there, also, for his Christmas leave, & he wishes to be remembered to you.

We had to leave there early, as our train left at 7-30, & we arrived back in Mansfield about 8-15. To-day I am Orderley Corporal again; so you see, darling, it is the only little bit of Christmas I've had. I think it is about the worst Christmas I have ever had, but then you see, darling, I have been very busy also. However, I can look forward to a week to-day, my beloved, & also to the lovely time, you & I are going to have together. I am so sorry you got into trouble over being out singing on Christmas Eve; but you see my darling you might easily of caught cold again & we don't want you down with illness again. Still, I suppose you knew best, beloved, although in my humble opinion I don't think you ought to have gone. I am glad you liked the Chocolates, but you must not thank me for them, darling. I am only to pleased to be allowed to send them. I was rather surprised to learn that Harry Taylor had got married, but that would account for the worried look, as you say, sweetheart. It seems rather hard on them to have had their leave cut down to 24 hours, but we are living in a time of uncertainties at present, you know, beauty. We never know up here, from one day to the next, how we are working. It is an awful day here, to-day, & it is blowing a gale & raining in torrents. The Camp is in about 6 inches of mud & water & is in a terrible state. We never seem to be dry above an hour or two together. However, it's all in the game so we mustn't grumble, must we? I am glad that Gladys came to see you, & hope that you both had an enjoyable day to-gether yesterday. It would feel quite a change for you both. I had a letter from Ma by the same post as yours & she seems to be getting on alright, but does not say when she is coming home. But perhaps she will be letting me know later. I hope you will have a good time at the Social to-day; but for pity's sake don't recite any of my stuff. Please spare the long suffering public as much as you can darling. And now, my beloved, I must be coming to a close

once again. So good-night my darling & pleasant dreams.
PS Give my love to Mother & all at home. H.

Just a line or two to say that I received a letter from Ma by
yesterday's post & she came home last Tuesday; so perhaps
you will be going up to tea to-morrow (Sunday). Willie has
got a week-end pass again, until Sunday night, so you may be
seeing him either to-day or Sunday. I do not know that I have
any special news this time, but it is New Year's day to-day & I
wish the usual 'Happy New Year' & I hope it will be a better
one than last year both for you & for me, my beloved. I am
coming home on Monday (as far as I know at present) but I am
afraid it will be late, darling, as the train doesn't leave Mansfield
until 5-30. However, I expect to be in Huddersfield about 11
o'clock, but if I am any earlier, I will come on. If not, then I
will see you on Tuesday at 12-30, unless of course you will
come to meet me. But I think it will be a little too late, darling,
for a pretty little girl to be out. However, we shall see. I think
this is about all this time, but give my love to Mother & all at
home. Hoping to see you before long.

Just a short note to say that I am very, very sorry to have
to disappoint you again, but I cannot get home to-day as
promised; but hope to be with you either to-morrow (Tuesday)
or Wednesday. The reason is, that we have sent a draft of 50
men to the Battallion this morning,[90] & as you can guess, all is
disorder & confusion in the Camp. Hoping that I have not to
disappoint you again, sweetheart,
PS Give my love to Mother & all at home. H.

FROM HENRY, CLIPSTONE CAMP, 6 JANUARY 1916

Just a line or two to say that I am sorry I have kept you waiting so long for a letter; but I have been expecting to come home on pass every day, but have not got off yet. I don't know the reason why we have not gone yet, but I expect it's 'slacksetupness' on somebody's part or other. You know the Army (like the Law) moves very slowly; so you must not lose heart darling; but I expect to come home sometime this year (or next.) However, beauty, the latest rumour this morning, is that we are going to-morrow (Friday) but I will send you a Telegram when we *do* actually get off. I don't know that I have anything special this time, but I think I am going on alright. In the meantime you might drop me a line or two to-morrow & let me know how you are getting on darling.

PS Give my love to Mother & all at home.

FROM HENRY, CLIPSTONE CAMP, 8 JANUARY 1916

Just a few lines to say that I received your welcome loving letter by yesterday's post & was glad to hear from you. I am sorry you have been so terribly disappointed at my not coming home during the last few days & that you have been put to so much inconvenience, but you will know the reason now, by the last letter I wrote you the other day, sweetheart... I am so sorry that you dropped the Cash Drawer on your foot, sweetheart, but hope you are better by now. I am writing this to you on Saturday night & I do feel so lonely somehow without you, my beloved. It seems ages since I saw you last, although it is only a month ago; but you know it is because I love you so dearly that the time seems so long. I am afraid that I have missed the post here, to-night, so it will probably be Monday before you receive this, as to-morrow's post does not leave until 5-30 at night, being Sunday. I am enclosing you two new Gladys Coopers & hope you will like them. Also a few Cards for the Boys...

FROM HENRY, CLIPSTONE CAMP, 10 JANUARY 1916

Very many thanks for your loving welcome letter which I received by this morning's post. I wrote to you on Saturday night, but I don't think you will have received it until this morning, as the Sunday post from here does not leave until evening. Percy has come to Clipstone to rejoin the Hudd'd 3rd /5^{th91} : so Willie & I went with him to Alfreton again to his young lady's; & had our tea there. I do hope you won't mind, darling, but it does feel nice to get out of Camp, even if it's only for a half day. I was telling her about you & she said she would like to meet you; she was sure you must be nice. I said you was the sweetest & dearest, loving little Girl in all the world; which is more than nice beloved. I have come off Orderley Corporal, at last, but have been firing on the Miniature Range all day, so feel just a bit tired to-night. We are having a visit from the Lord Mayor of Leeds to-morrow, & having our Photos taken for the Cinemas^{92}; so I suppose we ought to feel highly 'flattened.' I am Corporal of the Guard again to-morrow morning until 9–30 Wednesday morning; so I look like having a pic-nic. But we shall get over it & be as bad as ever. I have not heard anything further about our leave; but I suppose we shall have to rest our 'souls' in patience & hope for the best… Will you send me an 'Examiner' & a tin of Brown Polish, darling, for I am all about without? I do not know that I have any more fresh news; but give my love to Mother & all at home.

FROM HENRY, CLIPSTONE CAMP, 11 JANUARY 1916

Just a few lines to-night as promised, to say that I have not gone on Guard as expected. I got all ready, but was told at 9–30 that I should not be wanted, to-day, so I didn't feel sorry. Well darling, we have had the Lord Mayor up & the Cinema Man, as arranged, & I think all went off alright. He took us at Bayonet

Fighting, Swedish Drill, With Full Pack & Rifle (as on a Route March) & also at Boxing, Football, & Dinner; so I think they will be a few more 'smiling faces' on the 'Gaumont Graphic' next week.[93] But you will be able to read all about it in the 'Leeds Mercury' to-morrow, I expect. Willie & I are down at Mansfield to-night, & I am writing this at the Y.M.C.A. there. We came down to go to the 'Empire,' but we were too late, for it was 'House Full' when we got there. (I wish it had been Hudd'd Palace instead sweetheart, & that you were with me.) I think it is about time they got a 'move on' with our 6 day's leave, now. Don't you darling? …

FROM HENRY, CLIPSTONE CAMP, 16 JANUARY 1916

Just a line or two to say that I am coming home to-morrow (Monday) on my 6 day's leave; all being well. I do not know the time, but if I should arrive in Huddersfield before 11 o'clock, I will come on. If not, then I will come to meet you on Tuesday dinner-time. Give my love to Mother & all at home.

FROM HENRY, CLIPSTONE CAMP, 23 JANUARY 1916

Just a few lines to say that I arrived back alright about 10-30 & found all serene. We had to change at Sheffield & Worksop, but had to wait about an hour at both places, so that is why we were so late getting back, sweetheart. Willie is alright & has had a letter from Gladys, giving him an account of our visit to Ossett last Wednesday, & also going to the 'Empire;' so I couldn't tell him much about that, could I, darling? I have been to Chapel Parade this morning & am down at the Y.M. at Mansfield, with Willie & Percy, as I write this to you; this afternoon. It is just 4 o'clock, my beloved, I can just picture you at home with Ma. How I wish I was with you again, darling. Just to kiss & love you in the old sweet way. But there, I mustn't complain; for we have had 6 lovely days, my wife to be, & I think we shall both be a little better for having had them. Willie says he thinks he is coming home in about three weeks time; so I dare say you will be seeing him, when he does come. I am just in the same Hut yet darling, but have been transferred to 'C' Co. as you will see by the heading. We have had 60 Derby Recruits[94] come up since Thursday & are expecting more this next week; so I expect we *shall* have a time. I hope Mother & Father are better again, & continue to be so. And now, my beloved, I must be coming to a close as it is nearly tea-time. But keep a stout heart, don't worry, & all will come right in the end...

FROM HENRY, CLIPSTONE CAMP 25 JANUARY 1916

Just a few lines in reply to your loving welcome letter which I received by this morning's post. Also the small piece of Cardboard which I found quite safely. I will try & get a ring the same size, darling; but will not send one until I get a real good one. Although you have become engaged to me, my beloved; I don't feel that I am quite good enough for you; for you are so lovely & sweet in my eyes. Still, I am *quite certain* that I love you (& worship you) more than life itself; & that I try to live up to you daily; my own. Also, that you love me in return; so I am quite certain that we shall be very, very happy together when we do get married. (Which I hope will be in the near future.) Although this might seem a serious letter, my wife to be, it is just like I feel to-night, as I write this to you. (Oh, & I *do* love you, my beauty.) I am so sorry that you feel so lonely, darling, but I feel just the same without *you*. It always takes me a day or two to settle down again, & I suppose it will take you the same. But you see we are all in all to each other; so that is the reason. I am glad that you went home on Sunday (& it is *your* home too) & hope Ma is alright. I wrote to her last night (Monday) but I have not yet had a reply. I have been on Bombing[95] again this

Ring gauge, with the 'O' size measurement cut out. This is the gauge that Henry used to ascertain Lucy's finger size so that he could buy her an engagement ring.

morning & a short route march this afternoon; but we have a 20 mile march to-morrow (Weds.) with full pack & Rifle. Also, the Derby Recruits are going as well, so what a Picnic?

FROM HENRY, CLIPSTONE CAMP, 2 FEBRUARY 1916

Very many thanks for your loving welcome letter which I received by last night's post. I was very, very sorry to hear that Miss Crowther has passed away; but I had heard from Ma that she had been very ill. I can guess that Ma will be very much upset over it, dear. I do not know that I have anything special to tell you, darling, but I suppose you will have read in the Papers about a Zepp. Raid on Sheffield, Tye Bridge & Nottingham, on Monday night. They passed over at about 3 miles from here & our Sentries say they heard them very plainly, when they were on guard. I had a letter from Teddy last Sunday morning, (he is at North Shields by the way) but I am enclosing it for you to read. It will give you a good idea of how he is getting on. I am on duty at the Firing Range this week, from 7 o'clock in the morning, until 3-30. It is right on the moors, about 5 miles away from Camp, & I have all the Ammunition to deal with & check; so you can guess that I am pretty busy when I have 1200 rounds each day to deal with. Willie left here on Monday for his 6 days leave, but perhaps he & Gladys have been to see you this (Weds.) afternoon. He said he was going to take you out, on your afternoon off, darling. I wish I was over at home with you too, my beloved, but never mind sweetheart, I hope to be with you in a fortnight or so. I have not seen Alfred since the Sat. night I came back with him, but I ran across Freddy Chapman on the range last Monday. He says they are all going on alright, however. I do not know that I have anything more this time, sweetheart, but you might send me an 'Examiner' if you will darling. So goodnight, my wife to be, & God bless you for the sweet little Girl you are. Love to all at home.

With my fondest love & kisses, I remain, yours for eternity, Henry.

FROM HENRY, CLIPSTONE CAMP, 3 FEBRUARY 1916

Just a line or two to say that I duly received your letter, (written at Collinson's Café[96] yesterday) when I came off the range at 3-30, this afternoon. It came by this morning's post & you appear to have been having a good time & no error. I think I shall have to look to my laurels, darling, because (as you said in one of your letters) it is 'Leap Year;' & there might be a prospective marriage between a dear dainty damsel who resides at Tanfield Rd., & a budding 'recruit' at Cleveland Rd.[97] And then I should have to marry Gladys for consolation & live at Ossett I suppose. But putting joking on one side, my beloved, I am glad that you had a good time & hope you enjoyed the Palace at night. I do not know that I have anything fresh, after my letter of last night, but I am still busy on the Range. It was on Orders last night, that Lce/Sgt[98] F Crosland (Willie's brother) is to come to Clipstone from the Battallion, so I am expecting him here in a few days. The Battallion[99] went out to France last Sunday night, & arrived at Boulonge (The Base) on Tuesday morning, where they are to stay for a month or two. I am still keeping my Diary, darling, & hope you have got yours up to date by now, my beloved. I am enclosing you a parody which was written by _____. But there, you must guess, you beauty. I think this is about all this time, sweetheart, so must come to a 'finis' once more. Don't forget to give my love to Mother & all at home.

With my fondest love & kisses, I remain, yours for eternity, Henry. PS [Numerous kisses] On account. To be paid in full when I see you again. H.

[ON SEPARATE SHEET:]

We are Fred Karno's Army,
We are a Rotten Lot,
We are no good at shooting
What earthly good are we?
And when we get to Berlin
The Kaiser he will say:-
'Hoch! Hoch! Goot Got!
Got strife this lot
And send them all away.'
If you sing this to the tune of 'From Greetlands[100] Icy Mountains', you will get a very fair result. H.

FROM HENRY, CLIPSTONE CAMP, 5 FEBRUARY 1916

…I am going to see the 'Dream Girl' at the Grand Theatre to-night, all being well, & will let you know how I like it. (I wish

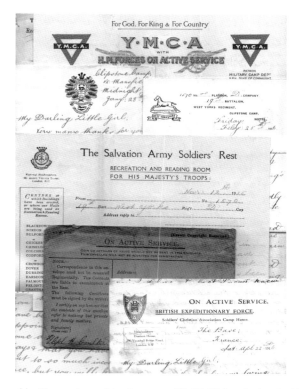

Notepaper used by Henry when writing from camp. The YMCA and other charities provided such paper free, but Henry would have had to pay for the paper with the Regimental badge.

it was the 'Shop-Girl' instead: down the Old Lane.) I should enjoy it ever so much better & so would she. I am just longing to hug & kiss you again, my darling; but we shall have to wait & have patience a little longer, sweetheart…

FROM HENRY, CLIPSTONE CAMP, 9 FEBRUARY 1916

Very many thanks for your loving sweet letter which I received by last night's post. I am on Guard again to-day, so am writing to you in the afternoon, sweetheart, this time, instead of at night: so you can get it first post in the morning. Willie arrived back alright, late last Sunday night, & I have had a detailed account of last Wednesday's doings. (you know what I mean, you 'beauty'.) I am glad you liked the Gladys Coopers alright; but I wasn't certain whether you had two like them, already. However, I was lucky. I received the letter (from Teddy) you enclosed, & thank you for it. So you think if you didn't marry me, beloved, you will marry no-one; & go and live in a Convent do you. I don't. You are far too pretty for that, darling, & I'm sure there are plenty fellows who would be only too honoured to marry you, if you would only have them. But there, my beloved, have no fear, for *I* love you far too dearly to lose you. I am glad you and Gladys went to Chapel with Ma last Sunday. Poor Gladys, I feel quite sorry for her. Willie would not believe Gladys had been to Chapel with Ma, until I showed him the letter. (but I covered the other parts up, you bet, darling.) It is a lovely day here, to-day, & your afternoon off too, beloved. How I wish I was with you instead of being on Guard. But duty first, my wife to be & then *you*. How do you like our Regimental Notepaper?[101] Not bad, is it? …

FROM HENRY, CLIPSTONE CAMP, 11 FEBRUARY 1916

…You must forgive me, beloved, for not writing you yesterday, but I have been rather busy since I came off Guard. I was on the Miniature Range yesterday afternoon, & we went trenching last night until 8-30. Then, when we got back, all the lights were turned out as more Zepps were reported about, so we had all to go to bed out off the way. It has been an awful day here to-day, darling. Snow & slush galore. We are over the ankles in it, when we turn out of the huts. I am enclosin[g] you a P.C. which I hope you will like. Also a Cig. Card or two for the Boys. I am glad that your Cousin is going on alright & hope George is also. Willie is alright, but their Frank has not come home from Andover yet. I think he is coming on Monday. Well, darling, I don't know that I have anything fresh this time, as things are going on in the old sweet way; but you must excuse the scribble as the pen nib is awful.

FROM HENRY, CLIPSTONE CAMP, 19 FEBRUARY 1916

Just a line or two to-night to say that I came off Guard alright again, this morning, & am writing this to you in the Mansfield Y.M.C.A. I am enclosing you another Souvenir Brooch, sweetheart, which I thought you would like. It is the latest one out, & I only saw it for the first time this afternoon. I am sorry to say, beloved, that I have lost the small piece of Cardboard you sent me a little while ago, so am sending you another Card of Ring sizes, to choose from.[102] I know it is very careless of me darling; but don't be vexed 'Beauty.' It must have slipped out of the 'Diary' you gave me, which I kept it in. Please cut me another one out & send it on to me, darling, & I promise not to lose it again…

FROM HENRY, CLIPSTONE CAMP, 20 FEBRUARY 1916

Just a few lines in reply to your loving welcome letter which I received by this morning's post. Also the one which you wrote last Wednesday & which you addressed to 'C' Co. It found me alright, sweetheart. I am down at Mansfield again to-day beloved & am writing this to you at 8-30 precisely. Willie & Percy have been down here too, but they have gone back to Camp, as Willie has to be back for 9 o'clock. I have a late extension as it happens, so there is no hurry for me until midnight. We have all three been to Chapel to-night, (as well as this morning's Service at Camp) & have enjoyed it very much. It is a very large place something similar to Queen St.[103] Well beloved, & how have you gone on at Almondbury to-day I wonder. I am sure you will have been a success, because people used to tell me, in civil life, that you always are. But you must write & give me a detailed account of it, sweetheart. I had a letter from Ma, yesterday, in which she says that a certain young lady (of the name of Carrie) came to see her on Thursday night, & that she wishes to live at our home. I have replied to Ma to-day, saying that I would rather she didn't come, as I have a strong objection to anyone living at home, other than our dearest friends, & relations. Besides, I don't think it would be fair to you, beloved, irrespective of anything else, & that is quite sufficient in *my* opinion. You see, you lovely little girlie, that *you* (& *you* alone) count first in my estimation, & every other thing comes after. I had a letter from Teddy a little while ago & he seems to be going on alright; but it is my turn to write to him, which I shall be doing before long. I hope you will enjoy the 'Cinema Star' this week, darling…

FROM HENRY, CLIPSTONE CAMP, 23 FEBRUARY 1916

Very many thanks for your loving sweet letter, which I received by last night's post. Also the ring Card, Beauty, which I promise you not to lose again. I am glad that you liked the brooch, sweetheart, & that it arrived in good order, but you must not thank me for it, my darling. It is enough for me to know that you wear it for my sake, in daily remembrance. I am Orderley Corporal again for this week, beloved, so shall not be able to come home for this week-end as expected. I am very sorry to disappoint you again, but it cannot be helped, & we shall have to hope for better luck next week. Willie has gone to Leeds on escort to-day, but I am expecting him back to-night. He said he should try & get to see Gladys at Ossett, for an hour or two, if he could possibly do so, but she will be writing & letting you [know], if he does. It is your afternoon off again to-day, my beloved, & I wish (as usual) that I could be with you to spend it to-gether, as we used to do in the by-gone days. But never mind, darling, we will make up for it, when the War finishes. I have not heard anything more from Ma about Carrie coming to live at home, but cannot agree with you, my beloved, in what you say about considering your feelings. It *does* consider [sic – concern?] you, beauty, & nobody knows it better than I. Still I don't think she will come. (In fact, on second thoughts, I'm sure she'd better not.) With all due respect, of course, to the young lady. I'm glad you was a big success at Almondbury, sweetheart, because I knew you would be, before you went. I have remembered you to Willie, darling, & told him about Dick Fletcher being at home. He wishes to be remembered to you in return, sweetheart. And now, my beloved, I must come to a close, as there goes that blessed Bugle again.

FROM HENRY, CLIPSTONE CAMP, 25 FEBRUARY 1916 (WITH AN ENCLOSURE FROM WILLIE CROSLAND)

Just a line or two in reply to your loving letter which I received by yesterday morning's post. Also the packet of Cigarettes, which you so kindly sent, & which you know quite well, you little beauty, are always welcome. We have had about two feet of Snow, sent down to us here (from Heaven I suppose) & we have had to knock off for to-day, & start shoveling a bit, just to keep our hand in, I suppose. I had a letter from Ma, yesterday, & also two 'Examiners' this morning. She says she was expecting you up last night, but it was a wretched night here, darling, & I was wondering whether you went or not. I am glad you enjoyed the Pictures at the Palladium, on Tuesday night, sweetheart, but if you remember I saw 'Charlie at the Bank,' at the 'Picturedrome,' when I was home on my 6 days leave. It was very laughable too, darling. I am sorry your Cousin got 5 days C.B., sweetheart, although I couldn't help but smile when I read about it. Well darling, I am writing this to you on Friday night, & it is snowing again as usual. I have missed the post again, I expect, so I don't think you will get this until Sunday morning, beloved… Willie wishes to be remembered to you, & encloses you a note. (I am allowing him that privilege, although I don't usually allow anyone to write to the sweetest little girl in the whole world.) But he's an exception…

[Enclosure]
'Lu',
I want something to do for 5 minutes, so I have taken this opportunity. I was at Leeds on Wednesday but I had not the chance of going to Ossett. I arrived there at 1.30 am & had to leave at 6 pm so I had not much time. Well I had best close or else I shall be having a blowing up from Henry. Don't forget to write to Gladys.
Yours Willie.

FROM HENRY, CLIPSTONE CAMP, 4 MARCH 1916

Just a line or two to say that I have not been able to get home to see you this week-end after all. I am very, very sorry that I have had to disappoint you after being so expectant, beloved, but I could not possibly come, as you already know, my sweetheart. Besides we have a draft of 50 men standing by, ready for France at an hour's notice, so that is another reason, but you can depend upon it Beauty, I shall come as soon as ever I possibly can, you know that, my own. Willie is just as disappointed as I, but we have to make the best of it, sweetheart… I note what you say about the Corporation 'Roll of Honour,' & could not help but smile, but you must not waste your time looking for my name, beloved. It is only one amongst many, but I can just understand your feelings, my lovely little Girl.[104] … PS Will you send me some Dubbin on sweetheart, as I am entirely without. H.

Just a few lines to thank so very much for your lovely letter
& parcel which I received, quite safely, by this morning's post.
It is very, very good of you, beloved, & I cannot thank you
enough. I have read the 'Examiner,' sweetheart, & passed it over
to Willie. Well, beauty, we have just sent a draft of 50 men off
to the Front, & I have just come in, after cheering them off.
They have gone to London to-night, & then on to Folkestone
in the morning, so that they can cross over in the day-time. It
makes one feel rather queer, my beloved, & wish just a wee bit
that one were going too. But there, sweetheart, I want to see
my lovely little Girl again before *I* go. I am glad that you went
to see Ma on Monday night, darling, & that she is alright. It
is very kind & considerate of you, my wife to be, but it is just
like you. I see by the Paper too, that the 'Pearl Girl' is at the
'Theatre Royal' next week,[105] & wish that I could be with you
to see it, sweetheart, but I am afraid that cannot be. I have not
heard anything further with regard to the Week-end Passes; but
we shall have to wait & hope for the best. Well, darling, I think,
that I have told you about all the news at present, but we are
having awful weather here at present & we are up to our ankles
in slush every time we go out of the Hut.

Just a few lines in reply to your loving welcome letter, which
I have just received by to-night's post. I am glad that you
received the Chocolates etc. alright; but you must not worry
about me going out,[106] my beloved, because I shall be all right.
I am sorry that I gave you such a shock, but it is better that
you should know, isn't it, sweetheart? Willie is here, as I write
this to you, & he thanks you for your kind wishes, & wants to
be remembered to you in turn. Percy is here too & sends his

best regards. Willie has had a letter from Gladys to-night; & he goes out at 3 o'clock in the morning, all being well, sweetheart. I should have liked to have gone with him, my beloved, but I don't think I shall be so very long now. Well, beauty, I think I am doing very fair on the range, as I can score a bull at 400 yards, which is not considered so bad here. I am glad that you will come over to Mansfield, my beloved, & I will let you (& Ma) know the date as soon as I can. For myself I am simply delighted at going out, but am so sorry for you, my lovely little girl, for I know you will miss me terribly. But still, sweetheart, think how splendid it will be, to be able to strike a *real* blow at last, for home & *you* my beloved. I have not yet heard from Ma, darling, but hope to receive a letter in the morning. You must not take it too much to heart, darling, nor Ma either; for I promise to be carefull; & you will see that everything will turn out right in the end. I have sent Ma a Parcel to-day, containing the letters you have sent me at different times; but I do hope they won't go astray again, as they did at Tynemouth. Well 'beauty' I have missed the post again, but you will forgive me won't you? So goodnight, beloved, & God bless you.

With my fondest love & kisses, I remain, just Henry.

FROM HENRY, CLIPSTONE CAMP, 16 MARCH 1916

Just a few lines to-night in reply to your long loving welcome letter, which I received by this afternoon's post. Well, sweetheart, I have just seen Willie off, to do his little bit over the Channel; & feel real full up as I write this, beloved. Poor old Boy. He tried to bear up, but the tears would fall at the last minute. He is only 19 darling & I *should* have liked to have gone with him, just to keep an eye on him. There is another draft of 18 men going out from 'D' Company on Monday, but they are all privates, as we are very short of N.C.O.'s at present & cannot let any more go, until further orders. Then we have had notice from the War Office to go to Blythe in Northumberland, before the 24th inst. so we go next Wednesday. It is a little Town on the North East Coast, & is about 8 miles from Tynemouth, where I was during last October, if you remember, darling. We are going on Coast defence work for the present; so you can set your dear little mind at ease for a time at least. I really thought I should be going out on Monday, with the rest of the Boys, but it seems that fate has intervened again; & I am not to go. But I *should* like to have a real go, if only for your dear sake. I wrote to Ma last night & told her the news, & that she was to tell you, if you came up home to-night. I know you will both be delighted (& Mother too) at the news; but for myself I don't feel particularly pleased about it. But we shall have to wait & see how things sort themselves out. For the present I am still firing on the range (which is about 4 miles from Camp & right on the moors) & getting drenched daily. Still it's all in the game, so we mustn't grumble must we darling?... Will you thank Mother (for me) for her splendid wishes, darling, & tell her not to worry for I shall be all right; when I *do* go out? But I fail to see where the braveness comes in; for it's only what thousands of fellows have done before me...

FROM HENRY, CLIPSTONE CAMP, 19 MARCH 1916

Just a few lines in reply to your loving welcome letter which I received yesterday (Saturday) morning. Well beloved, I don't know that I have any fresh news to tell you; but I am still fairing alright on the range; & thank you very much, dearest, for your praise; but you know beloved you shouldn't, because I am amply repaid when I know I am doing my best for your dear sake. We have had to go on the range again to-day (Sunday) as we have been delayed during the week owing to fogs & rain, so have had to make up for lost time. We have been there from 8 this morning until three o'clock this afternoon; &

it makes it a hard day for Sunday, sweetheart. However, it's all in the game beauty, & it's better than being torpedoed, anyway. I think we are going to Blythe on Wednesday, darling, but I don't know for certain; but we are making preparations for leaving here at any time, so I guess it won't be long. We are sending another draft out of 18 men, to-morrow, but no N.C.O.'s, as we have only about half a dozen left; so I have escaped it again, darling; so that will please a certain little darling that I know. I went down to the Mansfield Grand Theatre on Friday night & saw Fred Kitchen's Company, 'Smile Please.' It was very good, sweetheart, but it would have been far better if you had been with me, my lovely little girlie…

FROM HENRY, CLIPSTONE CAMP, 23 MARCH 1916

Just a line to let you know that we are leaving here at Midnight to-night (Thursday) for Blythe so do not write again until you hear from me further. I will send you my new address as soon as possible.

With my fondest love & kisses, Yours in haste, Henry.

PS I am enclosing you a letter which I received from Willie last night. H.

FROM HENRY, VICARAGE FIELD CAMP, SEATON DELAVAL, NORTHUMBERLAND, 25 MARCH 1916

Just a line or two to say that we arrived up here alright, at 11 o'clock yesterday morning, after a very tiresome journey. We left Clipstone at 1 o'clock in the morning, so you see it took us 10 hours to reach here. We are encamped in huts about 3 minutes walk from the sea-shore, & it is a very pretty place, though only small. The Village is 5 minutes walk away, & we are also 3 miles from Blythe & 4 from Whitley Bay. I wish you were here too, beloved, for I think it would just suit you too, & we could have some lovely walks along the Sands. I am going on to Tynemouth this afternoon just to have a look at the old place again. The 'grub' is alright too, beauty, *real* Butter this time, not 'Maggy Ann.' (Margarine.) I think this is about all at present, darling, for I am very busy this morning but I will write you more next time. Give my love to Mother & all at home.

With my fondest love & kisses, I remain, yours for eternity, Henry.

My address is:-

(1570) L/Cpl. H. Coulter, 'D' Coy. 19ᵗʰ West Yorks Regt., Vicarage Field Camp, Seaton Delaval, Northumberland.

Henry embarked for France on 9 April. If he and Lucy continued to write as frequently as usual, there must be some letters missing here.

FROM HENRY, THE BASE, FRANCE, 22 APRIL 1916[107]

My Darling Little Girl,

Very many thanks for your loving welcome letter, which you wrote on Weds. & which I received at 8 o'clock last night. Oh, Sweetheart, I was glad to hear from you, for it seemed such a long time since I did, although it is only just over a week. I also received the letter from Ma, which you posted along with it, but I will write to her this afternoon. It is Saturday morning as I write this, & pouring with rain out here. In fact I never knew such a rainy Country as France, for when it once starts it goes on for about 48 hours at a stretch & never ceases in the meantime. It's marvellous to me how the tents stand it. I am glad that you are going on alright, beloved, & that you were up at home on Wednesday; but you are also a brave little Girl & I am proud of you, my darling. Thank you too, sweetheart for saying that you will be true & faithfull to me whilst I am out here. I know you will, my beloved, & I love you & worship you just as much as ever I did, for I know you love me in return. So keep smiling, sweetheart, & write as often as you can & I will do the same. I have not yet received the parcel you sent on Weds: but it may be coming any time. I am sorry you have been so long in receiving my other letters, but perhaps I shall be able to get them thro' quicker in the future, darling. Ma says, in hers, that she is going to Manchester to-day, so I shall have to write to her there. Well, I think this is about all at present, but give my love to all at home, & write back as soon as you can. With my fondest love & kisses, I remain, yours for eternity, Henry.

FROM HENRY, INFANTRY BASE DEPOT, FRANCE, 26 APRIL 1916

My Darling Little Girl,

Very many thanks for your long loving sweet letter, which I have just received by this morning's post. It is very, very good of you to write to me so often, beloved, & I thank you very much for being so thoughtfull. It is a great consolation to know, that although I am so far away out here in a strange land, trying to do a little bit for good old England's sake; you & Ma (and several others including Mother) are constantly thinking about me & praying for my return. But I am happy & contented in a way, & as free & careless as ever; although I seem to miss you more than ever, my lovely little girl. You will understand perfectly, darling, what I mean, I know. Well, sweetheart, to get on with the news. We had a visit last night from our friends the Germans, in the shape of a Taube.[108] It flew right over the Camp & dropped us a couple of 'Easter Eggs' (Shells) which flew all over the place when they burst. Fortunately they did no damage, but they made two holes big enough to get a horse & cart in, so you can immagine the size of them. I think we were very lucky, because there are tents all up & down the place; but they always were rotten throwers. The fellows are all grumbling because they were all wakened up by the noise, during the night, & they want to know when they are going to get the extra sleep to make up for what they lost during the night. Oh sweetheart, the spirit out here is fine, & you never hear a grumble except its about the grub occasionally. That worry's them far more than the Germans ever did. For myself, I slept through it all, & the boys told me about it when I wakened this morning. I am glad that you & Mother like the Cards I sent, & tell Mother that I shall be glad to hear from her at any time. I am also glad that you & Ma had that serious little talk last Sunday night, beloved, because it makes it so much easier for you, doesn't it, sweetheart? But although you are engaged to me, darling, I do wish that I had been able to have sealed it with a ring, before I came out here. But that cannot be helped now, & it will have to wait until I can get back again, I'm afraid. But we belong to each other, my beloved, & love each other so dearly, that it really doesn't matter for the time being. Still, at the bottom of my heart, I would have liked you to have had one. What do you say darling? I have not yet received the parcel you packed for me last Wednesday, but perhaps it will be hear in a day or so. Don't forget the Photo darling. Of course I remember the old lane, sweetheart, & we are going to have more jolly times down there, & also in the big arm-chair, when I come home again. So cheer up & 'keep smiling' as Mother says. I think this is about all again, this time beloved, but write back before long. So goodbye & God bless you my lovely wife to be.

With my fondest love & kisses, I remain, yours for eternity, Henry.

There is unfortunately another long gap in the correspondence here, at a time when Henry joined his battalion and first saw service in the front line.

My Darling Lu,

Very many thanks for your loving welcome letter, which you wrote on Friday Sept 8th, & which I received last Wednesday the 13th. You must forgive me for not writing earlier, sweetheart, but we have been in the Trenches again for six days & and only came out on Saturday morning, so that is the reason. However, both Willie & I came out again safely, but it is a very quiet part where we are now, in comparison to where we have been.[109] I received the parcel alright last Tuesday & am pleased to say that it arrived in very good condition this time. It was not even bulged, but I think it was due to your packing the different things, separately in linen. I think it is a very good idea, darling, & keeps the things much fresher. Many thanks for the Cigarettes, dear, & also for the little note you enclosed. I am glad that you had a good day in Leeds & that you enjoyed yourself. I am sorry to say that the man Foster (who called at home, whilst he was on leave the other week, if you remember) was taken ill in the Trenches & has had to go into Hospital, but I think he will be all right again before very long. Also I have just heard that Harry Watson is training at Yarmouth, so you see I can tell you a little bit of local news, yet darling. I have also just received the letter you wrote last Wednesday, to-day, & thank you for it. It is very good of you to write as often as you do, darling. We are having some very wet weather out here at present, & I am all about wet through as I write this to you, but it is all in the game so we can't grumble. We are having a few days rest at present & at a ruined little village just behind the line, & are billeted underground on account of the shelling. I am glad that you are on the Committee of the Y.M.C.A. & also that it is a great success. And now I must be coming to a close again as it is getting dark, but write back as soon as you can,

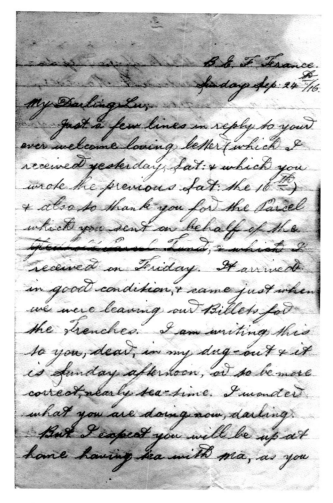

Letter written by Henry in a dug-out in the front line trenches, 24 September 1916. Written in pencil, it appears to be damp-stained.

darling, & tell me all the news. Also give my love to Mother & all at home, & tell her that I will write her before long. With fondest love; I remain, yours as before, Henry.

FROM HENRY, BEF, FRANCE, 24 SEPTEMBER 1916

My Darling Lu,

Just a few lines in reply to your ever welcome loving letter (which I received yesterday, Sat. & which you wrote the previous Sat. the 16th) & also to thank you for the Parcel which you sent on behalf of the Gledholt Parcel Fund which I received on Friday. It arrived in good condition, & came just when we were leaving our Billets for the Trenches. I am writing this to you, dear, in my dug-out & it is Sunday afternoon, or to be more correct, nearly tea-time. I wonder what you are doing now, darling. But I expect you will be up at home having tea with Ma, as you usually do on a Sunday. We are in the line until Thursday morning, but I am in the reserve Trenches this time, so you need have no fear, darling, for I shall be all serene. I was sorry to learn that you have had a Parcel returned from Egypt, intended for Frank Cowling; but it will just give you some idea of how the Parcels are knocked about & in what condition they sometimes arrive here, darling. I have not come across him yet, by the way, or Teddy either. With regard to your reciting at the Y.M.C.A. on Wednesday of this week; you are surely not going to inflict any of those old things of mine on a long suffering public, darling.[110] Besides, there's a War on dearest, & also think of your reputation as an Elecutionist. However, putting joking on one side, do as you like, darling, as I know you know best, but if you do say them, let me know how they go & also what kind of a reception you get. I am afraid that I have not much fresh news to tell you, but you might thank Mr Hall, on my behalf, for the Parcel from Gledholt. Also I am still going on alright & keeping in the best of health, so you must not worry darling. And now I must be coming to a close again as tea is all about ready, but write back as soon as you can & tell me all the news. With love to Mother & all at home.

I remain, with fondest love, yours as before, Henry.

YOUR PACKAGE ARRIVED ALL RIGHT A THOUSAND THANKS TO YOU.
Votre colis est arrivé à bon port, merci mille fois.

Postcard illustrating the delight Henry must have felt when he received a parcel from Gledholt Methodist Church, addressed by Lucy. (Private collection)

PS I received the usual Weekly Papers, yesterday, & thank you for them. H.

FROM LUCY, 27 SEPT 1916

My Darling Boy,

You will no doubt think I have been a long time writing to you again, but you see dear I have been waiting for a letter from you, and it has come at last though it has been delayed having been a week and a day on the way. You wrote it on Mon the 18th & I received it on Tues. the 26th. And oh I was so glad to get it dear for I wondered very much how you were getting on then Ma had a letter & I felt a bit better. I am glad you got the parcel alright dear & hope you have got the Gledholt one in good condition also, & the letter I sent about the same time. I was awfully sorry to hear about the illness of Mr Foster,

perhaps it was due to the change of life for a few days, I hope
he is alright again. Well dear I have been up to tea with Ma
today and tonight we have been to see Mrs Crosland, she is of
course very much upset because they have taken Harold for a
soldier,[111] and as she as not heard from Willie lately was rather
anxious until I told her that when you wrote me last he was
all right. I was rather surprised again dear to hear about Harry
Watson from you, Marion has been wondering where he was
training & was glad when I told her. Well Henry the Zepps
have been at Sheffield Monday night of this week & done
considerable damage, but not to any place of military value,
We were warned here and all lights were out & cars stopped,
but they did not pay us a visit for which I am thankful, though
how you manage to stand the constant bombarding day by
day without having a breakdown beats me.[112] Marion has been
to Sheffield with her boy for two days (that being his home)
and she just got home on the last tram to leave on Mon. night
before the raiding began. Her boy stayed until to-day however
& has had a terrible time as the bombs were dropped in their
district. Well sweetheart there is a rumour going about here
that leave from the front is starting again from most regiments,
is there any truth in it dear and are you at all likely to come
home Oh I do hope so dear for I want to see you again so
much. The Australians are coming on leave now there are quite
a lot of them in town & Mrs Cowling is expecting Frank home.
Your Aunt Eliza has been over this week from Manchester.
I saw her of course when I went on Sunday, but she went
home yesterday so I did not see her to-day. Well dear we had
a ripping week at the Palace here last week, and my old friend
Gus Harris[113] paid a return visit though in much better form
than when he was here last time, when you & I went to see
him. This time he sung 'I'm the only Jewish Scotsman in the
Irish Fusiliers' & 'Steadily Shoulder to Shoulder the Gentile

& the Jew' both of which took very well, he was really at his worst when you saw him. Oh I must not forget to tell you that Walter Waterworth has been home on Six days leave which he thinks will be his last, he came into our shop to see his uncle, on Saturday morning and asked how you was & where you were. I told him as much as I knew. Amy was at Blackpool when he came home, but of course was not long in coming home (I dont blame her). Emmie Crowther's boy has not to go for which needless to say she is very thankful. Well dear I don't think I have much more news this time I am sorry that you are having rainy weather out there it must make it awfull for you, I was so hoping there would be no winter campaign, but it seems as though there will be doesn't it dear. However I will hope for the best & look forward to your home coming. And now sweetheart Goodnight & God guard you through this night and for all time.

With fondest love & kisses, I remain Yours Untill death and beyond, Lu.

Mother, Father & the boys send their love. Lu.

FOUR FIELD SERVICE POSTCARDS[114], FROM HENRY, 27 SEPTEMBER, 30 SEPTEMBER, 3 OCTOBER AND 6 OCTOBER 1916

All state that Henry is 'quite well.'

Between the 5th and 11th October 1916 the 17th West Yorkshires were manning the trenches in 'K1' sector of the Arras front. There were no major attacks by the British or Germans during that period, although there were repeated warnings and cancellations received by the Battalion of a British gas attack. On the 10 October, Henry was badly injured. This happened when, as an acting Corporal, he was in charge of a working party.[115] It seems that an enemy trench mortar round exploded, causing the trench to collapse on top of him, an all too common occurrence. On this day the Battalion War Diary records the following incident, almost certainly the one in which Henry was hurt:

Field Service Postcard, one of four in the collection. This card, dated 6 October 1916, is the last surviving communication from Henry to Lucy.

17TH BATTALION WEST YORKSHIRE REGIMENT: WAR DIARY

10/10/16. Our artillery fire stopped hostile trench mortars about 4.30 pm. We suffered considerable damage however. Seven men were killed & two wounded, all in the vicinity of our Stokes emplacement. One heavy T.M. fell above entrance of 30 ft dug-out in VICTORIA ST. The entrance was completely demolished & filled in to within 5 feet of the bottom. The Lewis gun was destroyed by T.M. Work of clearing trenches blown in took considerable time, & much work was done in repairing them.[116]

FROM LUCY, 12 WESTBOURNE ROAD, MARSH, 22 OCTOBER 1916
Addressed to: (1570) Cpl. H. Coulter, c/o Sister G. A. Howe, (Sister in Charge), 37 Casualty Clearing Station, B.E.F., France.

Dearest Henry,
We are wondering how & where you are Ma and I, and are very anxious about you, not having heard since last Sunday,[117] which although only a week dear, to us anxiously waiting at home seems more like a month. I hope you got the short note that I enclosed in the sisters letter last week which I know by now must have reached her, but she has not written since last Thursday, although she promised to let us know what progress you made. Well dear I hope you are much better, & am hoping to hear that you will soon be in England or Blighty as you call it over there, then we can come & see you whereas at present we can do nothing but wait, hope, & pray, for your speedy recovery. You will no doubt be pleased to know that we have had two letters from Willie, he is still in hospital, & he was very much concerned about you, and asked us for your address. I wrote to him on Wednesday, and sent the only one we had, but perhaps you will have heard from him before the letter reaches you. We have had a letter from your Aunt in Manchester & she tells us that your father has had two telegrams from the War Office so we think he must have been making enquiries about you and they have told him that you could not be visited. You will be surprised to know that Teddy is in Northampton Hospital suffering from Contraction of the heart he has been there three weeks. Poor Teddy I did not think he would stand it

long. The man Foster got his brother to call & see us during the week, & he told us what he knew about your condition. Just now dear we are thankfull for news of you from any source. I have been here every night for a week staying with Ma for company or rather it's a case of company for each other dear untill we hear further news of you. And now I am going to stop (because patients have not to be unduly excited,) so for the present I will close, hoping to hear of you being this side before long. Ma sends her best love & hopes to see you soon, she would like to know if there is anything you want that we could send you & if it is at all possible dear will you please get someone to write & let us know how you are getting on. And now I must ring off for you must be tired so with fondest love & kisses I remain

Yours for eternity, Lu.

This letter is enclosed in an 'OHMS Returned Postal Packet envelope', with an instruction slip, and addressed to 'Lu', 12 Westbourne Rd, Marsh, Huddersfield. The envelope of Lucy's letter is marked in blue pencil:
'Died in Hospital before letter arrived. R [ ] Lt RAMC .'[118]

NEWSPAPER: HUDDERSFIELD EXAMINER 28 OCTOBER 1916 [119]

Page three contains notices and photographs of local casualties, including the following:

TRAMWAY CLERK'S DEATH FROM INJURIES
Corporal Henry Coulter, the nephew of Mrs Luke Schofield, with whom he resided at 12, Westbourne Road, Marsh, died of injuries in France on the 19th instant. Corporal Coulter was in the West Yorkshire Regiment, and early this month part of a trench fell upon him, causing fatal injuries. He was 24 years of age, enlisted in May 1915, and went to France last April.

Envelope of the letter Lucy sent to Henry when she heard that he had been wounded and was in a Casualty Clearing Station.

He was formerly a clerk at the tramway offices, and a member of the Gledholt Wesleyan Chapel Bible Class. His father, Mr Henry Coulter, resides at Manchester.

Henry was buried in an extension to the local communal cemetery at Avesnes-le-Comte, a village in the Pas-de-Calais about 20kms west of Arras. This cemetery was used by 37th Casualty Clearing Station from April 1916 to July 1917, as well as by other CCSs. A total of 333 soldiers are buried there, as well as two in the communal cemetery itself.[120] Henry was posthumously awarded the British War Medal and Victory Medal for his service during the Great War.[121] They were presumably sent to his father as next-of-kin, along with a bronze memorial plaque, bearing his name. These plaques were sent to the relatives of all men and women who died in the war.

Postscript

Following some publicity about these letters in the *Huddersfield Examiner*, I was contacted by a lady in New Mill, who possesses the diaries of her father, Stanley Charlesworth, who had served during the Great War in the Royal Army Medical Corps (RAMC).[122] Throughout the diaries for 1916, 1917 and 1918 there are mentions of Lucy Townend, with whom Stanley was obviously in love. His daughter had often wondered who Lucy was and was therefore amazed to open her newspaper and find a photograph of her! The owner of the diaries has generously allowed me access to them, so that a later chapter in the story of Lucy Townend's experience in the Great War can be told.

On 15 March 1916 Lucy wrote Henry Coulter a 'long loving welcome letter.' On that day she also went to the Huddersfield Co-op Employees' Social. There she met a 23-year-old Private in the RAMC, Stanley Charlesworth, a carpenter and joiner in civilian life, but now serving in the War Hospital at Royds Hall. Stanley courteously escorted Lucy home to Birkby, although his home was at Fisher Green, Honley. Over the next few weeks he took her on walks, to the pictures, and to an RAMC dance. He even showed her round the War Hospital. He met Lucy's Canadian cousin George, who was mentioned by Henry in a letter of 5 December 1915. Stanley was obviously smitten with Lucy, but we may doubt whether she felt the same way, since she continued to write lovingly to Henry.

On 14 April Stanley states in his diary 'Rec'd a sad letter from Lucy wishing me "good bye." Went for a walk to talk matters over. Had a very sad parting… Met Lucy on 15 March & courted her for four weeks & 2 days, then came the terrible blow when we had to part on 14th April.' This was of course the time that Henry had embarked for France. Lucy apparently felt that her loyalty had to lie with Henry.

Stanley continued to write to Lucy, and saw her sometimes at her shop. On 5 August he noted 'Went for a long walk with Lucy at night, and she told me all.' 'All' was presumably about her engagement to Henry. However, Stanley and Lucy continued to see each other occasionally, and on 26 August Stanley 'Gave her my RAMC cap badge which I had made into a brooch.' It will be remembered that Henry had also given Lucy two 'sweetheart brooches' made from his regimental badge.

Stanley himself embarked for France on 24 September, joining 15th Field Ambulance attached to the Fifth Division. On 10 October, the day Henry was fatally injured, Stanley was acting as a stretcher bearer with his unit elsewhere on the Front. He often wrote to Lucy, sometimes letters 2,000 words long, but Lucy's replies were far less frequent. On 4 January 1917 he notes 'I received a nice letter from Lucy. She told me her Canadian cousin was wounded, & was in Hudds. War Hospital.'[123] On the 24th he received another letter in which 'She told me of the sad death of her friend. He died in the 37th CCS near Comby.' The 'friend' must have been Henry, since it was at this hospital that he had died, nearly four months before. Stanley continued to write long letters, but received few in reply; at one point he complains of waiting about three months for a letter from Lucy. Many of his letters were sent in green envelopes – which he refers to as 'Green 'uns'. These army-issue envelopes were not subject to being opened and censored regimentally (although they were 'liable to examination at the Base'), and so could be used for private matters that the writer would not want seen by his regimental officer. A 'very disappointing' letter from Lucy in November suggests that she was still less serious about the relationship than Stanley, and perhaps still mourning Henry. A week's leave in Huddersfield was marred by Lucy's mother who had been 'making her miserable, but she promised to meet me on Sunday in spite of her mother.' On the evening of the 22nd they went to the Picturedrome and for a short walk, 'but we were both rather sad.'

In December Stanley's division was sent to Italy to help repel attacks by the Austrians. Letters from Lucy were still rare despite Stanley's writing 16-page missives – and poems. However, after his return to the Western Front, on 30 April 1918 'I received my very best love letter from Lucy and she told me for the first time that she loved me.' Lucy's parents were still against the relationship; perhaps they felt it was too soon after Henry's death, or they did not want to see their daughter's heart broken by the loss of another soldier boyfriend. In July therefore Lucy wrote that 'it must be goodbye… through her parents.' Much to Stanley's relief, they soon relented and 'consented to our happiness.'

Although as a medical orderly Stanley was not engaged in actually fighting the enemy, he was nevertheless often in danger, taking his turn in the forward first aid posts, rescuing wounded from the battlefield, enduring heavy shell-fire. An illustration that a 'non-combatant' role was not an easy option is shown by the diary entry for 28 June 1917:

> We were afterwards attached to the Norfolks and had no cases till 5 pm when Fritz bombarded our support lines and we were soon overflowing with wounded, and our Aid Post was swimming with blood and we were like butchers and we were carrying continually for 14 hours.

The effects of the war came even closer to Stanley and his family when, on 29 September 1918, his brother Roy, serving with the 1/5th Bn South Staffordshire Regiment, was killed in action.[124] Roy had been courting Doris Gamble, who lived in Birkby Hall Road; she and Lucy seem to have been friends. Lucy sent Stanley a 'fine letter of condolence.'

By this time the German army was in retreat, but bloody fighting continued to the bitter end. Happily for Stanley, he was granted leave on 6 November, so that he was actually in Huddersfield on 11 November, when the Armistice was declared. His diary entry for that day reads:

THE GREAT WAR FINISHED. HOSTILITIES CEASED AT 11 O'CLOCK. GREAT REJOICING. I had tea at Magdale. Lucy troubled.

Over the next few days Lucy continued to be very sad, even 'brokenhearted.' Was she thinking of Henry, and perhaps also of all her other young friends who had died – Willie Crosland, dead the previous year, or the other nine young men from Gledholt Methodist Church whose names would appear alongside Henry's on the church's war memorial. She did recover sufficiently to accompany Stanley on visits to his relatives, and to the cinema, before Stanley returned to France on 21 November. On 7 January 1919 Stanley sent a 'Green 'un' to Lucy from Belgium. And there the story ends. His diary for 1919 has not been traced and there are no further mentions in later diaries. At some time Stanley and Lucy's romance came to an end. In 1931 Stanley married Ann Sykes of Linthwaite.

Eventually Lucy must have been reconciled to Henry's loss, as so many young women had to who lost husbands or sweethearts in the Great War. In 1924 she married a local man in Huddersfield, and enjoyed a long and happy marriage, with two children and several grandchildren. One of her brothers inherited the house in Tanfield Road, and after both he and Lucy had lost their spouses, Lucy moved back to live with her brother. She died in North Yorkshire in 1982. It is a matter of speculation when she bundled up the letters in the newspaper that announced the death of her sweetheart, and hid them in the attic: probably in 1916 when she was a teenager grieving for her Henry.

Appendix 1:
17th (Service) Battalion West Yorkshire Regiment

This battalion was one of the 'Kitchener battalions' raised from volunteers called for by Lord Kitchener, Minister of War, to meet the needs for huge numbers of infantry for the fighting on the Western Front. The Battalion was also known as the '2nd Leeds' to distinguish them from the 15th Battalion or Leeds Pals. Their more usual name however was the 'Leeds Bantams.' Bantam battalions were raised from men who were too short to meet the original physical requirements of the army, normally not below 5 feet 3 inches in height. After objection from men who were short but otherwise fit and wanted to fulfil their patriotic duty, a battalion was raised in Birkenhead and called 'Bantams' after the small but fierce type of chicken. Men had to be between 5 feet and 5 feet 3 inches in height, with a chest measurement of at least 34 inches. Many other regions followed this lead. It therefore seems that Henry Coulter was rather short, and that is why he joined a Leeds unit rather than a Huddersfield one.[125]

The Leeds Bantams were organised and paid for by the Lord Mayor and City of Leeds in December 1914. In June 1915 they were assigned to 106 Brigade of the 35th (Bantam) Division, along with the 17th Bn, Royal Scots (Edinburgh), 19th Bn, Durham Light Infantry (Hartlepool) and 18th Bn, Highland Light Infantry (Glasgow). They trained at camps near Ilkley, Skipton, Masham, Chiseldon, Perham Downs (near Salisbury), Larkhill, and back to Perham Downs. From there they entrained on 31 January 1916 for Southampton, embarking the same day for Le Havre. They were commanded by Lieutenant Colonel F N J Atkinson.[126] The first elements went into trenches on 20 February; during this training period they lost two men killed and two wounded. Over the next few months they moved around various sectors of the Western Front, taking part in no major battles, but nevertheless sustaining many casualties. For example, between 13 and 31 July they lost ten officers and 304 other ranks (out of a nominal strength of about 1,000). One source describes the conditions experienced by the battalion at this time:

> The spell in the front line invariably meant very strenuous work, much of which arose from the persistent manner in which the enemy blew the trenches in with heavy trench mortars. When relieved, the battalion took up positions in the rear, and spent the next six days providing working parties to assist in maintaining the front line trenches, wire, etc.[127]

This was the situation at the time Henry Coulter was fatally injured.

At the end of 1916, it was decided that the 'Bantam' concept could not be maintained, since it was found difficult to keep up the supply of men with the necessary physical specifications, and many of the small men (and under-aged boys) recruited had proved unable to cope with the strenuous demands of trench warfare. The Battalion War Diary notes on 13 December 1916:

> Received notice that ADMS wd. inspect Bn on 14/12/16 with a view to weeding out unfit men. Letter from Div. stating that in re-organising Bn. C.O. must disregard "Bantam" standard & that standard of efficiency must be that of other Divisions of the Army.

Many of these unfit men were discharged, and full-sized men drafted in instead.

A member of the 15th (Leeds Pals) Bn, West Yorkshire Regiment rather unkindly remarked:

> The Bantams were a nuisance. They couldn't help being little men, but at the same time, when they stood on the firestep

[in the trenches], they couldn't see over! We filled a sandbag full of soil and let them stand on it. Not only that, when the Germans knew they were [in] they came over, because I think they wanted one or two as souvenirs.[128]

This account of the modification of trenches for the small men was not an exaggeration. When the Bantam Division first entered the trenches, the following order was given:

Two sandbags per man for filling and placing on the fire-step will be provided... Parapets are not to be lowered.[129]

OVERHEARD ON THE SOMME.

Red Hat—" What's the circus, Jock ?
Guide—" Bantams, from Cork ! "
Red Hat—" S'truth, shove 'em inside th' barn and bolt the door, or the cats will get at 'em. '

Cartoon mocking the small size of Bantams soldiers. This was drawn by a patient at the War Hospital, who had presumably come across Bantams in the trenches.
(Huddersfield War Hospital Magazine 1917)

The 17th continued to sustain many casualties during minor attacks and raids during 1917. During a raid on the German trenches by three officers and 100 men on 17 April the Battalion lost eight wounded and ten missing – the latter dead or captured. Pte William Boynton Butler of the 17th won Britain's highest bravery award, the Victoria Cross, for an action on 6 August when he placed himself between his comrades and a live shell, shielding them from the explosion, in which he was injured. On 31 August the 17th was the target of a 'minor' enemy attack, in which the 17th sustained two officers killed, five missing and six wounded, and seven other ranks killed, 53 missing and 56 wounded.

On 14 July 1917, Henry Coulter's friend Willie Crosland was killed, probably during a German attack on the battalion in the Epehy sector, accompanied by shelling.[130] At the end of 1917 the huge losses sustained by the army meant that brigades were reduced from four to three battalions each, in order to make the other battalions up to strength. The 17th Battalion was amalgamated with the 15th Battalion West Yorkshire Regiment (Leeds Pals), a total of seven officers, four sergeants, five corporals and 260 privates being contributed by the 17th. The combined battalion was designated the '15th/17th.'

During its service from February 1916 to December 1917, the 17th Battalion lost a total of 16 officers and 270 men killed or died. There is a brass plaque in memory of the Battalion in St Peter's Parish Church, Leeds.

Appendix 2:
Selected people mentioned in the letters

AINLEY, HERBERT MCARTHUR. Son of Law and Margaret Ainley, 24 Regent Road, Edgerton, Huddersfield. 3185 Pte, 1/5th Duke of Wellington's Regiment. Died 17 Nov 1915, aged 21. No known grave – commemorated on the Ypres (Menin Gate) Memorial, and Gledholt Chapel memorial. [CWGC].

'ARTHUR' An Arthur Chapman is named on the Gledholt Chapel memorial as a survivor.

BATES, HARTLEY Killed.

BEARTON, PERCY (?) 3/5th Bn Duke of Wellington's Regiment.

BLACKSHAW, MISS Worked in the same shop as Lucy.

BOWER, HARRY 21, 'Henry J Bower' named on Gledholt Chapel memorial as a survivor. Harry and Lawrence were possibly the sons of Albert Bower (died 1948), a local preacher for sixty years, as well as acting as caretaker and as an official of the Gledholt Circuit Temperance Society and several other offices. [Shaw and Free, *Gledholt Methodist Church,* p 13; A J Shields, *Sixty Years 1888-1948: The Story of the Gledholt Circuit, Huddersfield* (Birkby, 19148 p 16.]

BRIER, WILLIAM ('WILLIE'). 956 21st Bn West Yorkshire Regiment. Died 6 May 1917. Buried Fauborg d'Amiens Cemetery, Arras. Named on Gledholt Chapel memorial. Herbert Brier, possibly a brother, is also named on the Chapel memorial as a survivor. [CWGC].

BUCKALL, CAPT H S 17th Bn West Yorkshire Regiment. Commissioned 28 Dec 1914. At the end of the war he was a Major in the 11th Bn East Lancashire regiment. [*Monthly Army List* (Dec 1919) p. 1037a.]

CHAPMAN, FRED. Son of Fred and Mary Hannah Chapman, 136 East View, Lee Mount, Halifax. Born Marsh, Huddersfield. Mentioned as in Leeds Rifles, but presumably transferred later, as he is listed as 202261 Pte, A Coy, 2/4th Leicestershire Regiment, died 19 April 1917, aged 20. Buried in Peronne Communal Cemetery extension. Named on Gledholt Chapel memorial. [CWGC]

CHARLESWORTH STANLEY RAMC. From Fisher Green, Honley. Formerly a joiner and carpenter. Later friend of Lucy Townend.

COWLING, FRANK Cyril, Frank and Raymond Cowling are named on the Gledholt Chapel memorial as survivors.

CROSLAND, FRANK Brother of Harold and Willie. Lance Sergeant, 17th Bn West Yorkshire Regiment.

CROSLAND, HAROLD Brother of Frank and Willie. In the army.

CROSLAND, WILLIE Friend of Henry and Lucy. Son of Henry Hirst Crosland and Mary Hannah Crosland, of 921 Manchester Road, Linthwaite, Huddersfield. Brother of Frank and Harold. Lived at Cleveland Road, Edgerton, Huddersfield. 19/146 L/Cpl, 17th Bn West Yorkshire Regiment. Died 14 July 1917 aged 19. Buried in Templeux-le-Guerard British Cemetery, 26 km east of Peronne. [CWGC]

CROWTHER ('Emmie Crowther's boy'). Robert H and Stanley Crowther are named on the Gledholt Chapel memorial as survivors.

DAWSON, — From Aspley, Huddersfield. 17th Bn West Yorkshire Regiment. Worked at Brown and Thomas.

ELIZA [NEÉ COULTER] Henry's aunt, living in Manchester.

FLETCHER, 'YOUNG' DICK Royal Field Artillery.

'GLADYS' From Ossett. Willie Crosland's girl-friend.

HALL, MR Connected with Gledholt Chapel.

HEATON, HARRY No details.

HICKMAN, MRS From Gledholt Chapel. George F Hickman, possibly her son, is named on the Chapel memorial as a survivor.

HOLLAND, FRANK No details.

LILLEY, ALFRED Leeds Rifles. Named on the Gledholt Chapel memorial as a survivor. 'LITTLE WILLIE' See Crosland, Willie.

'MARION' Worked in the same shop as Lucy. She had a boy-friend in Sheffield (possibly Harry Watson, q.v.).

NEWSOME, ARNOLD E Named on the Gledholt Chapel memorial as a survivor.

'PERCY' See Bearton, Percy.

PORTLAND, DUKE AND DUCHESS OF Owned the land on which Clipstone Camp was built; spoke to Henry Coulter during a visit to the camp.

ROSCOE ERNEST 2nd Lieut 17th Bn West Yorkshire Regiment. Died as a result of a road accident 26 June 1915.

SHAW, HERBERT Named on the Gledholt Chapel memorial as a survivor.

SHEARD, BERTIE No details.

TAYLOR, HARRY From Huddersfield.

THORPE, BERTIE Presumably George Herbert Thorpe: Son of Thomas Henry and Jane Middlebrook Thorpe, of Huddersfield. 2787 1/5th Duke of Wellington's Regiment. Died 17 Nov 1915 aged 22. Buried in Talana Farm Cemetery. Named on Gledholt Chapel memorial. Alfred H Thorpe, possibly a brother, is also named on the memorial as a survivor. [CWGC]

WATERWORTH, WALTER E Nephew of Mr Waterworth. Gunner, Royal Garrison Artillery. Named on the Gledholt Chapel memorial as a survivor.

WATERWORTH, MR Worked in the same shop as Lucy; uncle of Walter.

WATSON, HARRY Marion's boy-friend? In the army.

'WILLIE' See Crosland, Willie.

Appendix 3:
War Memorials and Rolls of Honour

In Gledholt Wesleyan Methodist Church there is a Roll of Honour comprising a wooden wall plaque painted with the words

> To the Glory of God, Gledholt Wesleyan Church Roll of Honour and in Honour of those who served in the Great War this tablet is dedicated.

In the centre is a brass plaque inscribed

> In ever loving memory of those who gave their lives 1914-1919.
> Herbert Ainley
> Arthur W Bailey
> William Brier
> Fred Chapman
> Henry Coulter
> Arthur Jackson
> Percy Liddell
> Wilfred Morgan
> George H Thorpe
> Ernest P Wilton
> "Their name liveth for evermore."

On each side of this plaque are painted the names of other members of the church who served in the war and survived, as follows:

Herbert Armitage	Wilson Hirst
Jack L Armitage	Stanley Holdsworth
Ronald Armitage	Jack H Humphreys

John Bevers
Austin K Bottomley
Henry J Bower
Laurence Bower
Herbert Brier
Fred Cartwright
Arthur Chapman
Richard J Clarke
Norman Clayton
Cyril Cowling
Frank Cowling
Raymond Cowling
Albert Crampton
Robert H Crowther
Stanley Crowther
Norman Dodgson
Ephraim Dyson
John Archie Elliott
James O Elliott
Robert Elliott
Arnold Eyre
Thomas L Grosvenor
Herman Haigh
Harry Harvey
Geo E Hickman

Herbert Iredale
William H Iredale
Fred Kitchener
Stanley Lever
Ernest Liddell
Alfred Lilley
Dyson Mallinson
Geo D Mallinson
Vincent Milner
Ernest W Moore
Arnold E Newsome
Tom Pearson
Herbert Shaw
Henry Small
Hubert Smith
Clara L Thornton
Norman W Thornton
Philip Thornton
Alfred H Thorpe
Harold F Waite
Arnold L Walker
Geoffrey Walker
Walter E Waterworth
Harry Whitebread
Harold B Wilkinson

Henry Coulter's name is also included on the bronze war memorial on the main staircase of Huddersfield Town Hall, which lists Huddersfield Corporation employees who died in the two world wars. Also displayed in the main corridor of the Town Hall are two illuminated manuscript Rolls of Honour, listing all employees of the Corporation who served in the Great War. Henry's name is listed in the Tramways Department section. During the First World War

The Roll of Honour in Gledholt Methodist Church. The names of the ten men killed are on the brass plaque in the centre; those who survived war service are listed on either side.

at least 678 men from the Corporation joined the armed forces, of whom 53 were killed, and 54 wounded.[131]

Henry's aunt Adeline – 'Ma' – died aged 80 on 12 November 1939, at the start of another Great War. She is buried with her husband Luke Schofield in the south-west corner of Lindley Methodist Church's cemetery.[132] The inscription on the white marble stone, now prone on the grave, is almost illegible, but fortunately was recorded in the 1980s by local historian Edward Law. After the names and dates of Luke and Adeline, another name has been added:

Also Henry Coulter,
Nephew of Adeline and Luke Schofield, died of wounds
19th October 1916
and was interred at Avesne-le-Comte Cemetery, Arras.
At Rest.

Lucy Townend.

Henry Coulter. (Huddersfield examiner 1916)

Bibliography

UNPUBLISHED SOURCES

The National Archives (TNA):
WO 95/2490/4 War Diary of 17th Bn West Yorkshire Regiment.

WO 372/5/440080 Medal Index Cards.

West Yorkshire Archive Service:
RD/12/6/3-3 County Borough of Huddersfield Great War Roll of
    Honour.

Census 1901, 1911.

Huddersfield Local Studies Library:
Burgess Rolls, Huddersfield 1908–13.
Burial Registers, Edgerton Cemetery.
Burial Registers, Lindley Methodist Church.
Marriage Registers, Almondbury Parish Church 1924.

Huddersfield Examiner.

PUBLICATIONS

S Allinson, *The Bantams* (2nd edn, Barnsley, 2009).

Owen Balmforth, *Jubilee History of the Corporation of Huddersfield
    1868 to 1918* (Huddersfield, 1918).

S Chadwick, *The Mighty Screen: The Rise of the Cinema in Huddersfield*
    (Huddersfield, 1953).

R E B Coombs, *Before Endeavours Fade* (4th edn., London, 1983).

H M Davson, *The History of the 35th Division in the Great War* (London, 1926).

Du Ruvigny's Roll of Honour 1914–1924 Vol 2.

J S Farmer, *The Regimental Records of the British Army* (London, 1901).

H Fisher, *Record of Service: 168th Brigade RFA* (Huddersfield, 1946).

Marie Hartley and Joan Ingilby, *Life and Tradition in West Yorkshire* (London, 1976).

F Nigel Hepper (ed), *Captain Hepper's Great War Diary 1916–1919* (South Stainmore, 2011).

Kelly's West Riding of Yorkshire Directory (1917).

London Cigarette Card Company, *The Complete Catalogue of British Cigarette Cards* (Exeter, 1981).

L Magnus, *The West Riding Territorials in the Great War* (London, 1920).

P A Margetts, Letter. *The Briggensian* (Magazine of Brigg Grammar School) Vol 1 No 4 (Easter Term 1915).

Pauline Marples, *Clipstone Camp and the Mansfield Area in World War One* (Mansfield, 2013).

Laurie Milner, *Leeds Pals* (Barnsley, 1998).

Cyril Pearce, *Comrades in Conscience: the story of an English community's opposition to the Great War* (London, 2001).

Robert Perks, 'Late Victorian and Edwardian Politics in Huddersfield.' In E A H Haigh (ed), *Huddersfield: A Most Handsome Town* (Huddersfield, 1992).

Roy Porter, *The Greatest Benefit to Mankind* (London, 1999).

David Raw, *Bradford Pals* (Barnsley, 2005).

Edward Royle, 'Religion in Huddersfield since the mid-Eighteenth century.' In Haigh, *Huddersfield: A most Handsome Town.*

Gill Rushworth, *Rushworth's Ltd of Huddersfield: The Story of a Department Store* (privately printed, Swaffham Bulbeck, 1999).

W H Scott, *Leeds in the Great War 1914–1918* (Leeds, 1923).

Christine Shaw & Lynn Free, *Gledholt Methodist Church 1890–1990* (privately printed, 1990).

A J Shields, *Sixty Years 1888–1948: The Story of the Gledholt Circuit, Huddersfield* (Birkby, 1948).

Peter Simkins, *Kitchener's Army: the raising of the New Armies 1914–1916* (Barnsley, 2007).

True North Books, *Nostalgic Memories of Huddersfield* (Huddersfield, 2011).

War Office, *Monthly Army List* (Dec 1919).

E Wyrall, *The West Yorkshire Regiment in the War 1914–1918* (2 vols, London, 1924 & 1927).

WEBSITES

http://www.britishpathe.com/video/lord-mayor-of-leeds/query/ COLSTERDALE (accessed Nov 2013).

http://www.clipstonecamp.co.uk (accessed Dec 2013).

http://www.cwgc.org (Commonwealth War Graves Commission website) (accessed various dates 2013-13).

http://www.monologues.co.uk/musichall/Songs-S/Sergeant-Solomon-Isaacstein.htm. (accessed June 2013).

Endnotes

1 *Du Ruvigny's Roll of Honour 1914–1924* Vol 2 p. 80. This entry was probably written by Henry's father.

2 The house was in Marsh Fold, adjacent to Gledholt Methodist Church. The Fold was demolished in 1961 to make way for the ambulance station that now occupies the site.

3 Morthen is a village 4½ miles south-east of Rotherham.

4 *The Fatal Thirteen, or, The Man with the Thumb* was a 'penny dreadful' story of brigands and heroes, written by Stephen H Agnew and published in 1902.

5 Quinsy is an abscess at the back of the throat, a complication of tonsillitis.

6 Note the reference to wartime censorship; Henry had presumably seen this phrase stamped on the envelope of letters sent by friends in the forces. Henry composed several monologues, some of which were included in the collection of his letters.

7 Dinner in Northern usage is the mid-day meal.

8 'Dreadnought' was their pet cat, presumably named after the revolutionary British battleship launched in 1906.

9 Francis, Day and Hunter, and Feldman were publishers of popular songs.

10 'Rushworth's Corner:' Rushworth's was a department store founded in 1875, and was originally situated on the west side of Market Place. In 1887 it moved to the corner of Westgate and John William Street, gradually expanding along both these streets. Rushworth's was sold to Hurst and Sendler of Leeds in 1966, but 'Rushworth's Corner' is still remembered by older people as a convenient place to meet in Huddersfield. [G Rushworth, *Rushworths of Huddersfield Ltd: the Story of a Department Store* (privately printed, Swaffham Bulbeck, 1999).]

11 Henry worked as a clerk in the Huddersfield Corporation Tramways Department.

12 The 1912 Huddersfield Trade Directory lists John Shaw, boot and shoe maker, at No 8 Westgate. In 1914 he joined in partnership with Elliott Hallas. Shaw and Hallas, with origins going back to 1864, are one of the oldest businesses still in operation in Huddersfield, although now in different premises. [True North Books, *Nostalgic Memories of Huddersfield* (2011) p. 45.]

13   David Raw, *Bradford Pals* (Barnsley, 2005) pp 75—6; W H Scott, *Leeds in the Great War 1914—1918* (Leeds, 1923); S Allinson, *The Bantams* (2nd edn, Barnsley, 2009).

14   Henry's first letter as a serving soldier.

15   These were the army's general-purpose food containers known as dixies — an Indian word.

16   Raw, *Bradford Pals*, pp 59-77.

17   Other names included North Pole, Buckingham Palace, and Sycamore — the last named after an unpopular officer called Moore. [Raw, *Bradford Pals*, p. 61.]

18   'Pack drill' was a punishment involving quick marching up and down with a full pack.

19   The Palace Theatre of Varieties, in Kirkgate, Huddersfield, was Henry and Lucy's favourite, to judge by the number of times they mention it. [*West Riding Directory* (1917) p. 1417.] It still stands, but was completely rebuilt in 1937. 'Cinemas, music halls, the Hippodrome and the variety theatres functioned vigorously throughout 1915. Their programmes were often laced with war-related items, either war films and newsreels, patriotic sketches or recruiting addresses.' [C Pearce, *Comrades in Conscience: The story of an English community's opposition to the Great War* (London, 2001) p. 88.]

20   'Little Willie' seems to be Willie Crosland (see list of people). Since he too later joined the Bantams he must have been quite short.

21   Swedish drill: A type of physical exercise (PE). A member of the 15th 'Pals' Battalion, West Yorkshire Regiment, at this time stationed at Colsterdale camp (where Henry himself was later stationed), described how 'At 6.30 we fall in on the Parade Ground for Swedish drill. At first this parade was not so strictly attended to as it should have been; but now sterner measures have been taken, and the parade is under the supervision of the Company Officer... The exercises are similar to those "inflicted" on the boys at school, although much harder.' [Letter 21 March 1915 from P A Margetts, printed in *The Briggensian* (Magazine of Brigg Grammar School) Vol 1 No 4 (Easter Term 1915) p. 6.]

22   The local newspaper, the *Huddersfield Examiner*, still in print.

23   'Sweetheart brooches', in the form of the regimental badge, were a common gift from soldiers to wives, girlfriends and mothers. The White Horse of Hanover was the badge of the West Yorkshire Regiment as a whole, not just the 17th Battalion. The badge, granted in 1765, was not the oldest 'mascot',

but Henry's regimental pride is understandable. [J S Farmer, *The Regimental Records of the British Army* (London, 1901) p. 105.]

24   Greenhead Park, just across the road from Gledholt Church, hosted regular band concerts; the bandstand has been recently restored to its Victorian splendour.

25   Colsterdale Camp.

26   It is uncertain what this anniversary was; the stone-laying and opening of the church were in October 1889 and 1890 respectively, so it was not related to the foundation of the church itself. The building seated 700 people; since many of these would have been children, £50 was an impressive sum.

27   P.O.: Postal Order, a common way to transfer small sums of money when few people had bank accounts.

28   William and Henry Heaton's tobacconist shop was situated at 8 Kirkgate and 72 John William Street, Huddersfield. [*West Riding Directory* (1917) p. 1419.]

29   Henry is never explicit about why he enlisted, but presumably it was for patriotic reasons. There was considerable opposition to the War in Huddersfield, mainly led by labour organisations, but also including several Methodist churches, notably those at Paddock and Lindley. Gledholt church does not seem to have been involved in the anti-war movement. As a Corporation employee, Henry would have been promised his full wages less his army pay whilst he served, with the promise that his post would be kept open for him when he was discharged. [Pearce, *Comrades in Conscience*, pp 131-2, 195-6.]

30   Henry enclosed a newspaper cutting about the duties of a postman 'being discharged temporarily by a woman' in Skipton, an example of women taking over jobs traditionally done by men.

31   Putties: strips of khaki cloth which were rolled around the lower leg. With the huge expansion of the army, items of uniform were in short supply and tended to be issued on an *ad hoc* basis. The mills of the Huddersfield district produced much of the khaki cloth. Sadly there is no photograph of Henry with the letters.

32   R.F.A.: Royal Field Artillery. This probably refers to the 168th Brigade, which was raised in the Huddersfield district.

33   'Enemy aliens' i.e. German-born civilians, were interned on the Isle of Man.

34   The Palladium Theatre was situated at the corner of Blacker Road and Leslie Street, Birkby, thus being close to Lucy's home. It was opened in 1914, with 500 seats, and closed in 1937, being rebuilt and reopened as

the Carlton. The building is now occupied by a mosque. [S Chadwick, *The Mighty Screen: The Rise of the Cinema in Huddersfield* (Huddersfield, 1953) p. 112.]

35   This probably refers to the Flag Day held in aid of wounded soldiers, which took place on Saturday 26 June 1915. It included a procession, a variety concert, and an inspection of 168th Brigade RFA in Greenhead Park. Perhaps Lucy was one of the 'young ladies selling sweetmeats and fruit' in the Market Place. The event raised nearly £1,000. [*Huddersfield Examiner* 28 June 1915.]

36   The Band of Hope was a temperance organisation aimed especially at working-class children. In 1904 the Huddersfield Band of Hope had 12,000 members. [Robert Perks, 'Late Victorian and Edwardian Politics in Huddersfield.' In E A H Haigh (ed) *Huddersfield: A Most Handsome Town* (Huddersfield, 1992) p. 510.]

37   'up home:' It is quite a steep climb up Blacker Road going from Lucy's home in Tanfield Road to Westbourne Road.

38   Henry enclosed a newspaper cutting reporting a car accident involving officers of the Battalion who were returning from an outing to the cinema in Ilkley. Second Lieutenant Ernest Roscoe died on 26 June, the first officer fatality in the Battalion. He is buried in Lawnswood Cemetery, Leeds. [E Wyrall, *The West Yorkshire Regiment in the War 1914–1918* (London, 1924) Vol 1 p. 308.]

39   Henry likens his complaints to a recorded message. The Edison Bell Company, named after the two most important inventors of recorded sound systems, marketed records in the UK and Europe. At this time flat disc-shaped records were beginning to take over from wax cylinders.

40   These must have been regular trips for Lucy's father in his job as a chauffeur.

41   An area of Huddersfield around the canal basin.

42   Brown and Thomas are listed in Huddersfield Directories as painters and decorators with premises at 6 Spring Street.

43   From the 1870s cigarette manufacturers inserted cardboard stiffeners in the packets. These were printed with a wide variety of subjects in sets, which were eagerly collected by boys such as Lucy's younger brothers.

44   Russells: not traced; possibly an error for Rushworth's.

45   Whitsuntide 'sings' or processions marked the end of Sunday school examinations, and were an especial feature of life in the West Riding of Yorkshire. They normally took the form of a procession of the children in their 'Sunday best' clothes, with decorated waggons, some carrying pianos.

At intervals the procession would stop and songs were sung. The event ended at a convenient field, where the children were given buns, lemonade and other treats. [Marie Hartley and Joan Ingilby, *Life and Tradition in West Yorkshire* (London, 1976) pp 94-6.]

46   6th (Territorial Force) Battalion, Duke of Wellington's (West Riding) Regiment, recruited from the Skipton, Settle and Keighley area.

47   This suggests that they had been issued originally with obsolete rifles, probably the Long Magazine Lee Enfield introduced in 1899, and were now to be given the Short Magazine Lee Enfield, first introduced in 1907, and the standard British infantry weapon during the Great War.

48   Storthes Hall, near Huddersfield, originally a private estate, was at this time a mental hospital. It is now (2014) owned by the University of Huddersfield.

49   6th Battalion, West Yorkshire Regiment.

50   *The Chocolate Soldier* was a light opera by Oscar Straus, based on Shaw's play *Arms and the Man*. It was first staged, in translation, in Britain in 1909, but Henry may be referring to the film which was released in 1915.

51   John W Leitch and Co had their chemical works in Milnsbridge, near Huddersfield. They were the first makers of the explosive TNT, in 1902. On Saturday 5 June 1915 heat from burning refuse caused a number of carboys (large glass flasks) of concentrated nitric acid to burst and ignite. The Huddersfield fire brigade, helped by the workers, managed to move several hundred other carboys to safety, dilute the acid, and disperse the dangerous fumes, with only minor injuries. The acid 'was ready for delivery to the War Office' – an example of Huddersfield industry's contribution to the war effort. [*Huddersfield Examiner* 7 June 1915 p. 2.]

52   Wills Cigarettes issued two series of cigarette cards entitled 'Overseas Dominions (Canada)' (issued from June 1914) and 'Overseas Dominions (Australia)' (issued from April 1915). Both showed views of the countries concerned. [London Cigarette Card Company, *The Complete Catalogue of British Cigarette Cards* (Exeter, 1981) p. 212.]

53   Huddersfield's Territorial unit was the 5th Battalion Duke of Wellington's (West Riding) Regiment.

54   Laurie Milner, *Leeds Pals* (Barnsley, 1998) pp 27-79, 225, which includes plans and an aerial photograph of the site.

55   P A Margetts of the 15th Bn West Yorkshire Regiment noted that meals were taken in the wooden Recreation Hall, which could seat 600 men. Breakfast consisted of coffee or cocoa, bacon or kippers, bread and butter, with sausages as an extra treat on Sundays. Dinner (at mid-day) was a pound

of meat and potatoes; if vegetables were supplied, there was no pudding (which was either boiled rice or 'roly-poly'). Extra food – coffee, buns, and tinned luxuries such as lobster and pineapple - could be purchased by those with money at the canteens, which were 'dry' i.e. did not sell alcoholic drinks. [Margetts, *Briggensian*, pp 6—7.]

56   Gladys Cooper (1888-1971) was a famous London-born star of musical and straight theatre, silent films, and later 'talkies' in Hollywood, in a career that spanned seven decades.

57   Hill 60 was a low but prominent artificial mound (resulting from nineteenth century railway construction) near Ypres. It was the scene of fierce and bloody fighting from April 1915 to June 1917. [R E B Coombs, *Before Endeavours Fade* (London, 4th edn., 1983) pp 46-7.]

58   A huge arc of camps was constructed around Ripon by April 1915, holding over 30,000 troops. [Raw, *Bradford Pals*, p. 82.]

59   War Horse Day was held in Huddersfield on 24 July 1915 to raise money for the Mayoress's fund for sick and wounded horses. 'From early in the morning until late at night a willing band of ladies and gentlemen were to be seen on the streets with collecting boxes and badges. Indeed, it was practically impossible to evade a collector…' There was also a procession of various floats and animals, including horses in slings and bandages, and a zebra from Halifax zoo. [*Huddersfield Examiner* 26 July 1915.] The Kirklees Museums collections include several arm-bands worn by collectors at various fund-raising days, including War Horse Day, and Poland Day. See also Lucy's letter of 9 August 1915.

60   Cigarette smoking (for men at least) carried none of today's worries about its effects on health; indeed some doctors argued that it was actually healthy. A woman smoking in public however would invite moral disapproval.

61   'Knut' was a term for a smart, fashionable young man.

62   By November 1915, twenty-five charities had been organised in Huddersfield, many of them to help refugees and other civilians affected by the war, in Belgium, France, Serbia and Russia as well as Poland. The money collected on Poland Day was sent to help those made homeless in the occupation by Austro-German forces. [Pearce, *Comrades in Conscience*, pp 88-9, 332 Note 6; *Huddersfield Examiner* 9 August 1915.]

63   Henry had been successful in obtaining a weekend pass on 14 August.

64   J H Scotland was a popular music-hall singer.

65   Dubbin: a brand of waterproofing for boots.

66   The 2/5th and 3/5th Battalions Duke of Wellington's Regiment. Such was

the demand for men, and response of volunteers, that Territorial battalions doubled and sometimes tripled in size, forming second and third line battalions. These were intended to be for training purposes, although many of the second line battalions (including the 2/5th Dukes) later served at the front. [L Magnus, *The West Riding Territorials in the Great War* (London, 1920) pp 69-77.]

67   4th (Territorial Force) Battalion Duke of Wellington's (West Riding) Regiment.

68   From 1915 a retiring collection was taken on the last Sunday of each month at Gledholt Methodist Church, to provide soldiers' comforts. Lucy obviously helped to pack up the parcels, as Henry mentions in one of his letters that he recognised her handwriting on the label. [Christine Shaw and Lynn Free, *Gledholt Methodist Church 1890–1990* (privately printed, 1990 p 12]. '16/=' is Lucy's abbreviation for sixteen shillings. In pre-decimal currency, there were twelve pence to the shilling, and twenty shillings to the pound.

69   Scarlet fever was a contagious streptococcal infection, often deadly to infants and young people. It only became less of a killer when living conditions began to improve towards the middle of the twentieth century. [R Porter, *The Greatest Benefit to Mankind* (London, 1999) p. 445.]

70   There are no surviving letters from Henry sent to Lucy in the sanatorium; presumably they were destroyed to prevent infection. The sanatorium was probably Mill Hill Isolation Hospital, used for cases of infectious diseases.

71   There were more than twenty bombing raids on Britain in 1915 carried out by Zeppelin airships, killing or wounding over 500 civilians. The first raid was on Great Yarmouth on 9 January 1915, when four civilians were killed and sixteen injured. In 1916, Gledholt Methodist Church and Sunday School were insured for £15,000 against damage from Zeppelin raids. [Shaw and Free, *Gledholt Methodist Church* p. 12.]

72   That is, their pet cat.

73   Gladys Cooper.

74   Fred Karno was the stage-name of the impresario Frederick John Westcott (1866-1941). His troupe of comedians at one time included Charlie Chaplin and Stan Laurel. 'Fred Karno's army' was a self-deprecating term popular with soldiers.

75   This was the music-hall singer, actor and comedian George Formby Senior (1875-1921), not his banjulele-playing son George Formby (1904-1961), whose stage career only started in 1921.

76   Tram car.

77   Disinfection due to Lucy's Scarlet Fever.

78   North Yorkshire Regiment.

79   In October 1915 Germany's ally Bulgaria attacked Serbia. To relieve this threat Britain and France sent an expeditionary force to Salonika at the end of the month. 168th (Huddersfield) Brigade RFA were training in Wiltshire at this time, but were not sent to Salonika. They joined the 32nd Division on the Western Front at the end of December. [H Fisher, *Record of Service: 168th Brigade RFA* (Huddersfield, 1946).]

80   A comprehensive illustrated history of the camp is contained in: Pauline Marples, *Clipstone Camp and the Mansfield Area in World War One* (Mansfield, 2013).

81   Apart from the Young Men's Christian Association huts at the camp, there were facilities provided by the Salvation Army, Church Army, the free churches, Wesleyan Methodists, and the Freemasons. There was also a YMCA hall in Mansfield, as Henry mentions. Many of Henry's letters were written on YMCA notepaper, which was provided free. Henry was not the only soldier writing home frequently: by the end of July 1915 the camp post office had dealt with 26,432 letters, 4690 postcards and about 100 parcels. [Marples, *Clipstone Camp*, pp 33-4, 46.]

82   7th (Territorial Force) Battalion, West Yorkshire Regiment.

83   A whole series of photographs of various parts of the camp was available for sale to the soldiers; many are reproduced in Marples, *Clipstone Camp*.

84   No doubt Gladys Cooper again. The postcard is not preserved in the collection.

85   The Duke and Duchess of Portland were visiting to open three YMCA huts. [Marples, *Clipstone Camp*, p. 46.]

86   The 'camp magazine' was issue No 8 of *The Growler*, the magazine of the 16th Bn Northumberland Fusiliers, for October 1915.

87   Henry had overstayed his leave.

88   Deo volente (Latin). Henry provides the translation.

89   The Picturedrome cinema was situated at 28 Buxton Road, Huddersfield. It was converted from a clothiers' premises, and opened in 1910. It closed in 1950, but reopened as the Curzon. At the outbreak of war in 1914 it gave free admission to Territorial soldiers in uniform. [S Chadwick, *The Mighty Screen: The Rise of the Cinema in Huddersfield* (Huddersfield, 1953) pp. 35, 112-3.] Later it advertised 'Admission FREE to [War] Hospital Patients, except Saturday and Bank Holidays.' [*Huddersfield War Hospital Magazine* August 1917).]

90 That is, a reinforcement of trained men had been transferred to the 17th West Yorkshire Regiment, which would soon be sent out to the front.

91 This was the 'Third Line' battalion, formed during the war to provide trained soldiers to the First and Second Line (1/5th and 2/5th) battalions of the Duke of Wellington's Regiment. The 3/5th Battalion did not therefore serve overseas.

92 That is, a movie film would be made to show at local cinemas.

93 A visit by the Mayor of Leeds to the Leeds Pals in camp was filmed by Pathé News; part of the film can be viewed on http://www.britishpathe.com/video/lord-mayor-of-leeds/query/COLSTERDALE (accessed Nov 2013). It is uncertain from the information given on the website whether the film was made at Colsterdale or Clipstone Camp. In either case, it gives a rare impression of the sort of event in which Henry participated at this time. Certainly it shows the troops equipped with 'Full Pack & Rifle.'

94 'Derby recruits' were not men from Derbyshire; the phrase referred to the 'Derby Scheme' introduced in October 1915 under the aegis of Lord Derby, which attempted to balance the needs of the army and industry, by calling up men in groups as they were needed, taking single men first. Call-up was based on a voluntary register of men aged 18 to 41, who were divided into groups according to age and marital status. It was replaced later in 1916 by conscription. [P Simkins, *Kitchener's Army: the raising of the New Armies 1914–1916* (Barnsley, 2007) pp 150-4.]

95 Bombing: grenade-throwing practice.

96 The café of T Collinson and Sons Ltd was situated at 30 and 32 New Street, Huddersfield. [*Huddersfield Directory* (1915-16) p. 74.]

97. A reference to Willie Crosland, who presumably was living at Cleveland Road, Edgerton, at this time – just around the corner from Gledholt Methodist Church. His parents lived in Manchester Road, Linthwaite, Huddersfield. [Commonwealth War Graves Commission Website.]

98 Lce/Sgt: Lance Sergeant, a non-commissioned appointment just below sergeant.

99 That is, 17th Battalion West Yorkshire Regiment. They embarked at Southampton on 31 January 1916, landing at Le Havre (not Boulogne) in France the next day. They then moved into camp at Harfleur. The Battalion formed part of 106 Brigade of the 35th (Bantam) Division. [Wyrall, *The West Yorkshire Regiment in the War,* p. 180.]

100   A pun on the local town of Greetland, and the well-known hymn-tune 'From Greenland's Icy Mountains.' Despite Henry's claim to authorship, versions of this parody seem to have been in wide circulation in the army.

101   It is embossed with the Regiment's badge. Willman's, stationers of White Hart Street, Mansfield, advertised 'camp stationary with Regt. crest' at this time. [Marples, *Clipstone Camp*, p. 80.]

102   Enclosed in this letter is the card ring-gauge, a replacement for the one mentioned on 25 January.

103   Queen Street Wesleyan Methodist Chapel, Huddersfield, was rebuilt in 1819 on a large scale, and could hold over 1,800 people. It is now the Lawrence Batley Theatre. [Edward Royle, 'Religion in Huddersfield since the mid-Eighteenth century.' In E A H Haigh, *Huddersfield: A Most Handsome Town* (Huddersfield, 1992) pp 106-7.]

104   Someone was apparently already compiling a list of all the Huddersfield Corporation employees who were serving in the armed forces. Henry's name appears on the illuminated Roll of Honour, which hangs in the foyer of Huddersfield Town Hall.

105.   The Theatre Royal was Huddersfield's oldest-established and premier theatre. At this period it was best known for its programmes of musical plays and comedies: 'The "Girls" in the titles alone present a baffling array. They include "A Country Girl," "The Cherry Girl," "The Girl from Kay's," "The Earl and the Girl," "The Girl in the Train," "The Girl in the Taxi," "The Quaker Girl," and a host of others. [S Chadwick, *"Theatre Royal" The Romance of the Huddersfield Stage* (Huddersfield, 1941).]

106   'Going out': that is, going out to join his Battalion on the Western Front.

107   This is first surviving letter from France. He does not say where 'The Base' is for security reasons; it may have been Boulogne.

108   Taube: the Etrich Taube, introduced in 1913, was the first major type of German military aircraft. It was used as a generic term for all German aircraft during the war.

109   The Regimental historian described the position of the Battalion at this time: 'Trench warfare of a more or less strenuous nature had occupied the 17th Battalion... from the middle of September, for the division, after leaving the Somme area at the beginning of August, had entrained north for the Arras sector of the line. The normal round of life in the front line, in support or reserve, was unrelieved by attacks on or by the enemy... [Wyrall, *The West Yorkshire Regiment in the War*, p. 302.]

110   Another reference to Henry's monologues.

111 'Taken… for a soldier': compulsory military service (conscription) had now been introduced, for the first time ever in Britain. Harold was Willie Crosland's brother. Their brother Frank was already serving in the army.

112 On the night of 25 September, a Zeppelin passed over West Yorkshire, being seen from Leeds. The large towns maintained an efficient black-out system; when a warning was received, electricity was turned off at the central generating stations, and gas pressure turned down to a minimum. This also meant that the tramcars stopped running and people caught out had to walk home! [Scott, *Leeds in the Great War*, pp 43, 163-71.] For air-raid precautions in Huddersfield see Vivien Hirst, *Family of Four: A Remembrance of Childhood* (Stockport, 1993) pp 149-50. As well as being involved in air-raid precautions, Vivien Hirst's father was active in the Huddersfield Volunteers, recruiting drives, and conscription appeal tribunals.

113 Gus Harris was a music hall singer, well known for his Jewish characters. The words to his song 'I'm the only Jewish Scotsman' are available on www. monologues.co.uk/musichall/Songs-S/Sergeant-Solomon-Isaacstein.htm.

114 As Field Service Postcards were sent openly through the post, only minimal information was allowed, in the form of crossing out from a range of statements any that did not apply. They were useful in quickly reassuring relatives at home, but were sometimes sent just before an attack in which a man might become a casualty.

115 *De Ruvigny's Roll of Honour 1914–1924.* Confirmation that this is the day Henry was injured is given in the County Borough of Huddersfield Great War Roll of Honour [West Yorkshire Archives Service RD/12/6/2-3] which was filled in by his aunt Adeline – 'Ma.'

116 TNA WO 95/2490/4. T.M.: trench mortar. Lewis gun: British light machine gun.

117 That is, 15 October; this was when they received a letter from the Sister at the Casualty Clearing Station, as implied in the next sentence. A letter or telegram giving news of Henry's injury would have been sent to Henry's father, as next-of-kin, and he or Henry's Aunt Eliza presumably wrote to tell Lucy or Henry's aunt the bad news.

118 Lieutenant, Royal Army Medical Corps. The name is illegible.

119 This newspaper was found wrapped around the letters.

120 CWGC website.

121 TNA WO 372/5/440080 Medal Index Card.

122 He enlisted on 2 October 1915.

123   On 27 May 1918 a letter from Lucy told him about 'the impudent letter sent by her cousin.'

124   42545 L/Cpl Henry Le Roy Charlesworth, aged 23 years, son of Wright and Constance M Charlesworth of Fisher Green, Honley. The CWGC Website gives his date of death as 28 September, but the diary states specifically that he died in an advance near the St Quentin canal on Sunday 29 September. Roy had also served in the King's Own Yorkshire Light Infantry. He has no known grave and his name is commemorated on the memorial at Vis-en-Artois, Pas de Calais.

125   The *Huddersfield Examiner* of 4 August 1915, in an appeal for more recruits, informs its readers that 'for those whose height will not permit of them joining Lord Kitchener's Army or the Territorials another Bantam Battalion, attached this time to the famous Green Howards, whose headquarters are at Richmond, in Yorkshire, is now being raised.'

126   The diary of a young Leeds officer in the 17th Battalion has been published: F Nigel Hepper (ed), *Captain Hepper's Great War Diary 1916–1919* (South Stainmore, 2011).

127   Scott, *Leeds in the Great War,* p. 121.

128   Milner, *Leeds Pals,* p. 190.

129   H M Davson, *The History of the 35th Division in the Great War* (London, 1926) p. 9.

130   CWGC Website; Davson, *35th Division,* pp. 66-7.

131   Owen Balmforth, *Jubilee History of the Corporation of Huddersfield 1868 to 1918* (Huddersfield, 1918) p. 100.

132   Gledholt Methodist Church does not have its own graveyard. The Lindley Burial Registers and Survey of Memorials are accessible at Huddersfield Local Studies Library.